D1118044

LETTERS TO ST. FRANCIS DE SALES:
Mostly on Prayer

BY THE SAME AUTHOR

Moments in Catholic History

Traveling With Jesus in the Holy Land

Married Saints

The Doctors of the Church:
Doctors of the First Millennium

The Doctors of the Church:
Doctors of the Second Millennium

American Saints

Memoirs of a Catholic Journalist

The Mission and Future of the Catholic Press
(Editor)

LETTERS TO
ST. FRANCIS de SALES:
Mostly on Prayer

John Francis Fink

ST PAULS

Alba House

Library of Congress Cataloging-in-Publication Data

Fink, John Francis.
    Letters to St. Francis de Sales : mostly on prayer / John
Francis Fink.
      p. cm.
  ISBN 0-8189-0922-6 (alk. paper)
    1. Prayer—Catholic Church. 2. Francis, de Sales, Saint,
1567-1622. I. Title: Letters to Saint Francis de Sales.
II. Title: Mostly on prayer. III. Francis, de Sales, Saint, 1567-1622.
IV. Title.

  BV210.3 .F55 2002
  248.3'2—dc21

                               2002071169

Produced and designed in the United States of America by the
Fathers and Brothers of the Society of St. Paul,
2187 Victory Boulevard, Staten Island, New York 10314-6603,
as part of their communications apostolate.

ISBN: 0-8189-0922-6

Printing Information:

Current Printing - first digit   1   2   3   4   5   6   7   8   9   10

Year of Current Printing - first year shown

2003   2004   2005   2006   2007   2008   2009   2010

Contents

Introduction

Yes, it's true. The title of this book is indeed similar to the last book written by the great Christian apologist and imaginative novelist C.S. Lewis—*Letters to Malcolm: Chiefly on Prayer*. It proved to be an excellent way for Lewis to present his thoughts about prayer, writing letters to an imaginary friend. Lewis even gave Malcolm a wife, Jane, and a son, George, in order to make some points about prayer. He was so successful that many people who read the book thought that his imaginary friends were real.

My letters *are* to a real person, St. Francis de Sales. He was an expert on prayer. I am not. In these letters I simply want to give my impression about what St. Francis wrote about prayer. In this regard, I feel exactly as C.S. Lewis did. Before writing *Letters to Malcolm* he tried several times to write a book about prayer, and always gave up. As he wrote to Malcolm, "In a book one would inevitably seem to be attempting, not discussion, but instruction. And for me to offer the world instruction about prayer would be impudence." That's the way I feel about it. With these letters to St. Francis, I don't intend to tell people how to pray, but I do intend to write my reactions to what St. Francis wrote when he told people how to pray. I will also write my own thoughts—and include a few of my foibles—on the subject. Then I hope you, the reader, will think (meditate?) about what both of us wrote and come up with some thoughts of your own.

Why St. Francis de Sales? After all, many other saints wrote about prayer. Why not write to St. Ignatius of Loyola, for example, whose *Spiritual Exercises* have been training Jesuits, and many others, in the practice of prayer since the sixteenth century? Or St. Teresa of Avila or St. John of the Cross, two mystics who wrote about prayer for the Carmelites? Or Sts. Augustine, Aquinas, Bernard, Alphonsus, or many of the other Doctors of the Church who had a lot to say about prayer? Why pick St. Francis de Sales?

Because I think he made it a point to write for the average person in the pew, probably better than anyone except perhaps Thomas à Kempis in *Imitation of Christ*. St. Francis wrote his great masterpiece, *Introduction to the Devout Life*, for people in every walk of life and particularly for lay people. It's a practical guide for anyone who wants to improve his or her devotional life. He himself noted that "almost all those who have hitherto written about devotion have been concerned with instructing persons wholly withdrawn from the world or have at least taught a kind of devotion that leads to such complete retirement. My purpose is to instruct those who live in town, within families, or at court, and by their state of life are obliged to live an ordinary life as to outward appearances."

Another reason for choosing St. Francis de Sales is because he's one of my patron saints. My name is John Francis and I chose St. John the Evangelist and St. Francis de Sales as my patrons. St. Francis is also the patron of the Catholic press and of journalists, and I spent all of my adult life working for the Catholic press. As I note in my first letter, St. Francis and I are not strangers since I talk to him frequently. Who better, then, to write to about prayer?

Still another reason for writing letters to St. Francis is that *Introduction to the Devout Life* itself began as a series of letters he wrote to Madame de Chamoisy, a cousin by marriage. She showed the letters to a Jesuit priest, Father Jean Fourier, who urged Francis to publish them as a book. It was immediately recognized as a masterpiece of mystical and devotional literature and was translated into many other languages.

These letters are not commentary on the entire *Introduction to the Devout Life*, which was written in five parts. It's only the second part that's devoted to "Elevating the Soul to God by Prayer and the Sacraments." That's mostly what I will write about, although I'll quote some passages from the rest of the book when it seems appropriate.

Here is a thumbnail sketch of St. Francis de Sales. (You can read a fuller treatment in my book *The Doctors of the Church of the Second Millennium*, published by Alba House.) He was born on August 21, 1567 at the Chateau de Sales in Swiss Savoy, the eldest of thirteen children. His father was an aristocrat. His mother, who was only fifteen when Francis was born, began to teach him herself. As Francis grew, his mother was helped by the Abbé Deage, who served as tutor. When he was fourteen, Francis and Abbé Deage were sent to the University of Paris, where Francis enrolled in the College of Clermont, directed by the Jesuits. Under the direction of both Abbé Deage and the Jesuits, his spiritual life matured and he decided he wanted to give his life to God. He placed himself under the special protection of the Blessed Virgin and took a vow of perpetual chastity.

After six years at the University of Paris,

Francis's father sent him to the University of Padua where he studied jurisprudence for four years and earned his doctor of law degree at age twenty-four. He then returned to his parents' chateau and, for eighteen months, lived the life of a young nobleman.

Francis had decided to become a priest but, up to that time, had confided only in his mother and to a few intimate friends, including his cousin, Canon Louis de Sales. Eventually, though, he had to face his father who, he knew, would be vigorously opposed. Then it happened that the provost of the chapter of cathedral canons in Geneva died. Canon Louis de Sales thought that Francis could be appointed to that position, and, if so, it would help Francis get his father's approval to become a priest. The position was offered, Francis accepted it, and his father reluctantly consented. Francis was ordained a priest on December 18, 1593, at age twenty-six.

He undertook his duties as provost of Geneva, but with headquarters in Annecy rather than in Geneva because Geneva was in Calvinist hands. Switzerland at that time was sharply divided along religious lines, especially in the Chablais, a section of Savoy along the southern shore of Lake Geneva where Protestants were in control.

Soon after Francis's ordination, Bishop

Claude de Granier of Geneva sought missionaries to send to Chablais. Francis and his cousin,
Louis de Sales, volunteered and the bishop accepted them. They set out for the Chateau des
Allinges, six or seven miles from Thonon, the
capital of Chablais. The chateau was a Catholic stronghold where the governor had a garri-
son of soldiers, so the two de Sales cousins had
to return there each night for safety. It was a
difficult life for the two cousins, especially in
winter when they had to make that walk to and
from Allinges every morning and night in
Switzerland's weather. On two occasions, Protestants waylaid Francis, intending to kill him.
His escape both times apparently was miracu-
lous.

Francis tried every way he could think of
to reach the minds and hearts of the people, and
it was at this time that he began writing leaflets
about Catholic doctrine, comparing it to the
teachings of Calvinism. These little papers, laboriously copied by hand and distributed by
any means available, were the beginning of
Francis's work as a writer. Later they were collected and printed in a volume called *Contro-
versies*.

Soon there was a stream of lapsed Catholics seeking reconciliation with the Catholic
Church, and Francis felt safe enough to leave
the Chateau des Allinges and live openly in

Thonon. He preached in the marketplace and had public debates with some of the Calvinist leaders in the area.

In 1597 Pope Clement VIII asked Francis to go to Geneva to debate Theodore de Beza, a distinguished Calvinist scholar. Francis was unable to bring Beza back into the Catholic Church, but the debate did bring many others back.

After several years, Bishop de Granier visited the mission and was amazed at the progress Francis and Louis had made. The bishop was considering a successor and recommended Francis as coadjutor bishop. Pope Clement VIII made the appointment.

Early in 1602, Bishop de Granier sent Francis to Paris to discuss the French section of the diocese of Geneva with King Henry IV, who had recently asserted his sovereignty over all France. The king was so impressed with Francis that he tried to persuade him to remain in France, but Francis declined. He also was invited to preach a series of sermons in the Chapel Royal at Paris to overflowing crowds.

Bishop de Granier died later in 1602 and Francis, then thirty-five, succeeded to the see of Geneva, with residence still in Annecy. He ran his household according to evangelical poverty and continued to preach and hear confessions. He promoted the teaching of catechism throughout the diocese and he himself gave instructions in Annecy. He also carried on a large correspondence in which he gave sympathetic guidance to many people. He practiced his axiom, "A spoonful of honey attracts more flies than a barrelful of vinegar."

In 1604 Francis met Jeanne Françoise Fremyot, the baroness of Chantal (later known as St. Jane Frances de Chantal), while he was preaching Lenten sermons in Dijon, France. Francis and Jane Frances founded the Order of the Visitation in 1610. He wrote his *Treatise on the Love of God* for the Visitation Sisters in 1616. A famous passage from that work is, "The measure of love is to love without measure."

He first published his *Introduction to the Devout Life* in 1609. During the next ten years he made revisions and published four more editions, with the definitive edition coming out in 1619. Perhaps his book can be summed up by a sentence that appears at the end of a paragraph in the thirteenth section of the fourth part of the book: "True devotion consists in a constant, resolute, prompt, and active will to do whatever we know is pleasing to God."

In 1622, Francis was at the Visitation convent at Lyons for Christmas. On December 27, he suffered a paralyzing stroke, but regained consciousness and his speech. He died the following day, December 28, 1622, at age fifty-five.

Francis was beatified by Pope Alexander VII in 1661, the first beatification to be held in Saint Peter's Basilica in the Vatican. He was canonized by the same pope in 1665, was declared a Doctor of the Church by Pope Pius IX in 1877, and named the patron of Catholic writers and the Catholic press by Pope Pius XI in 1923. The Church celebrates his feast on January 24.

I hope that this book will encourage readers to read the entire *Introduction to the Devout Life.* I recommend the edition edited and abridged for a modern audience by Msgr. Charles Dollen and published by Alba House.

LETTERS TO ST. FRANCIS DE SALES:
Mostly on Prayer

A Devout Life for All

Dear St. Francis,

I hope you don't mind my beginning a correspondence with you on the subject of prayer. After all, you and I are not strangers since I've been talking to you in my prayers for quite some time now, since I decided that I wanted you as one of my patron saints instead of some other St. Francis. You originally wrote *Introduction to the Devout Life* as a series of letters, and perhaps it's about time someone answered your letters.

Before getting to the subject of prayer, I must say that I have long appreciated your realization that, while not all Christians can practice their religion the same way, it's important that we all live a devout life. You said that true devotion "not only does no injury to one's vocation or occupation, but on the contrary adorns and beautifies it."

You, of course, were writing for the people

of the seventeenth century and you couldn't have imagined how hectic life would be in the future. Let me tell you that we in the twenty-first century are constantly on the go. One might think that modern conveniences might give us more time to turn to God in prayer, but it seems to be just the opposite. The Internet and cell phones put us in constant touch with others, and they can constantly be in touch with us. Never before, I believe, have we needed to learn how to pray as much as we do today.

There's another thing about life in the twenty-first century that I'm sure would surprise you. That's the role of women in our society. They no longer are restricted to work in their homes or to such occupations as nursing. Now young women grow up expecting to work outside the home in occupations as varied as those for men. At the same time, they also are expected to continue to bear the brunt of most housekeeping chores. These are conditions that your Philothea did not experience.

Perhaps it's just my imagination, but I believe that many people realize the need for prayer today and that the number of people who pray is growing. It's encouraging, in fact, that surveys indicate that most people do pray every day. I'm not sure that everyone has the same idea of what prayer is—and I wouldn't be at all surprised if most people pray prayers of petition almost exclusively—but at least people are praying.

One of the places I see more people praying is in our parish's Adoration Chapel. We are fortunate to have perpetual adoration at our parish, with people assigned to spend an hour at a time in the chapel before the exposed consecrated host in a monstrance—twenty-four hours a day, seven days a week, every day of the year except Good Friday and Holy Saturday. (People are welcome to pray on those two days but the consecrated host is removed.) Besides those assigned to certain hours, numerous other people stop in for visits throughout the day and night, as their schedules permit.

The people who come of the Adoration Chapel are as varied as those you described. There are doctors, lawyers, business men and women, married men and women, single people, mothers and fathers, the old, middle-aged and young. It really is quite inspiring to see such a variety of people.

All of these people undoubtedly realize, as you said, "that purely contemplative, monastic, and religious devotion cannot be exercised in their states of life." Most of those in our chapel weren't called to the religious life (although a few priests and religious are there at times). They live busy lives in the secular state (and life in the twenty-first century is secular indeed) and they understand their need for spiritual help as they go into the secular world.

I'm sure you would agree that people's prayer life can change—must change—as they age or their circumstances change. I'm putting it mildly when I say that I have considerably more time in which to pray today than I did during the years when our seven children were at home. I notice a big difference today when they come home and bring our grandchildren with them. I'm a person who likes routine; in fact, I think it's one of my faults that I'm not spontaneous enough: I establish a routine wherever I go for a few days. My daily routine, including my prayers, by necessity changes considerably when the family comes back home. And that, of course, is as it should be. I'm sure that's what you meant when you wrote that devotional life must be adapted to different states of life.

For those of us who are not in a monastery, routine is not always best and it's probably good for us to get chased out of our prayer routine from time to time. That's not an excuse, though, for living a less devout life or, as you put it, "aspiring to a perfect life." Even in the midst of the busiest lives (and I think that the busiest must be mothers of several children), we can aspire to a perfect life. Indeed, I agree with you (and I don't always agree with you, by the way) that "there have even been many cases of people who lost perfection in solitude, and have kept it in the midst of crowds, which seem to offer little help to perfection." By the way, I find those words comforting.

Prayer seems to be a universal action, a natural aspiration. We know of no culture in the history of the world that didn't include prayer of one type or another. Prayer is an important element of every religion be it Christian, Jewish, Muslim, Hindu, Buddhist, or whatever. Many of those religions have things to teach us Christians. Indeed, it's interesting that Thomas Merton, who knew and wrote a great deal about prayer, was trying to learn more about Eastern methods of contemplation before he died accidentally while he was in Bangkok.

Nevertheless, it seems to me that the Catholic Church has the most to offer when it comes to prayer. Above all, of course, it has the Mass, or the Sacred Liturgy, during which Jesus himself becomes truly present in the Eucharist. You, of course, agree with that, since you wrote a section on how to attend Holy Mass, and I'll write a separate letter about that later. But the Catholic Church offers much more besides. It offers the other sacraments, the Liturgy of the Hours, and devotions to the Blessed Virgin and other saints. It proposes certain rhythms of praying throughout the day, and its liturgical year, with its various feasts, provides opportunities for prayer. I'll also write more about all those things in later letters.

Conversation With God

Dear St. Francis,

You never did actually give a definition of prayer, but it can be inferred from the title you gave to the second part of *Introduction to the Devout Life*: "Various Instructions for Elevating the Soul to God by Prayer and the Sacraments." Elevating the soul to God does, indeed, seem like a good definition. The classic definition of prayer, though, is "the raising of the mind and heart to God in adoration, thanksgiving, reparation and petition."

Part of that definition comes from St. John Damascene who called prayer "the raising of one's mind and heart to God or the requesting of good things from God." That, I think, is what most people think of as prayer, especially the part about requesting good things from God.

Let me try another definition: "For me, prayer is a surge of the heart; it is a simple look turned toward heaven, it is cry of recognition and of love, embracing both trial and joy." That was St. Thérèse of Lisieux's definition.

I have to say, though, that I have always thought of prayer simply as a conversation with God or with the saints. We can talk about anything and our conversation can, and does, take the forms of adoration, thanksgiving, reparation and petition.

However we pray, the *Catechism of the Catholic Church* cautions us that "humility is the foundation of prayer. Only when we humbly acknowledge that 'we do not know how to pray as we ought,' are we ready to receive freely the gift of prayer." I don't make any claims toward humility (that would be a self-contradiction), but I readily admit that I don't know how to pray as I ought. That's one of the reasons I'm writing these letters.

(I hope you don't mind a parenthetical remark. Writing that last paragraph about humility made me think of the verse in the biblical Book of Numbers that says that Moses "was very humble, more so than anyone else on the face of the earth." Some people continue to believe that Moses personally wrote the first five books of the Bible. Moses indeed was humble and was able to converse with God often and at length, but I feel sure that he didn't write that verse about his being humble.)

We're agreed, I'm sure, St. Francis, that

God calls each of us to prayer. In fact, he always takes the initiative, as he did with Moses by speaking from the burning bush. What we do is to respond to God's initiative.

I have to tell you, St. Francis, that I'm disappointed that you didn't write more about vocal prayer. Instead, your very second paragraph on prayer and the sacraments says, "I especially counsel you to practice mental prayer, the prayer of the heart, and particularly that which centers on the life and passion of our Lord. By often turning your eyes on him in meditation, your whole soul will be filled with him."

Now, first of all, I think we can agree that all prayer is mental prayer because it involves, or should involve, thought and love of God. However, I think that you use "mental prayer" as synonymous with "meditation" because later you wrote, "Begin all your prayers, whether mental or vocal, in the presence of God," and in another place, "During vocal prayer if you find your heart drawn and invited to interior or mental prayer, don't refuse to take it up."

But I don't want to jump right to meditation. I want to consider vocal prayer first, and that for one principal reason: Most of the prayers of the Church are vocal prayers and I'm willing to bet that most people—even those in contemplative convents or monasteries—pray vocal prayers more often than they meditate. That is certainly true for me. I recognize that there are exceptions. C.S. Lewis was one. He wrote: "For many years after my conversion I never used any ready-made forms except the Lord's Prayer. In fact I tried to pray without words at all—not to verbalize the mental acts." But I think he was unusual.

We learn vocal prayer first, if we're lucky, from our mothers and fathers when we are first learning to speak: "God bless Daddy, God bless Mommy," the prayer to our guardian angel, and so on. Vocal prayer, of course, is the form of prayer that people say as a group, in a congregation or elsewhere. We use vocal prayer during liturgical celebrations, and Jesus himself taught his apostles a vocal prayer, the *Our Father*.

However, as I see it, St. Francis, the biggest problem with vocal prayer is that we too easily become distracted while saying prayers we have learned by rote. Our minds can be miles away while we continue to pray the prayers we have learned by heart. We're not thinking about what we're saying. We prattle on and on, saying prayers that are meaningful in themselves, while we think about all the things we have to do today or try to figure out how to solve that major problem in our lives.

This doesn't happen only with the traditional ready-made prayers such as the *Our Father, Hail Mary*, and other prayers we say frequently, but even with prayers we have made up that express our deepest emotions toward God. If we keep saying those same prayers over and over, they soon harden into a formula. I confess that this happens to me even while I'm praying after receiving Communion. I'm saying the most personal things I want to say to Jesus in this most intimate situation this side of heaven, all in my own words, but I've said them so often that they have become formulaic.

That type of praying isn't even good manners. It's like those people we've all known at cocktail parties who might be talking directly to us but who keep looking around at the other people in the room and aren't really paying any attention to us. When we're having our conversation with God, we certainly must make an effort to concentrate on what we're saying to him.

As far as I know, all we can do about distractions is to turn away from them, and toward what we are saying, as soon as we realize they are there. I'm not aware of any sure-fire method of completely eliminating distractions—I think they're simply part of our human condition—but we can force them out of our minds as soon as we're aware of them. A distraction indicates for us what we're really attached to, at least at the moment, and we know that we should be most attached to God.

Although we must make every effort to concentrate on our prayers, I can't believe that God is really offended when we allow distractions to get in the way. We are, after all, making an effort to pray. We have put prayer into our daily routine or we have taken up a prayerbook, breviary or whatever. Our intention is to talk with God and God knows (literally, since he made us) that we humans are easily distracted.

Can priests be expected to concentrate on the meaning of every prayer they say during the Mass? I'm sure they try to do so, and most priests say Mass devoutly, but after they have repeated the same words over and over for years, I'm sure that God is pleased that they are presiding at Mass with and for the people and he isn't going to mind if their minds stray a bit.

The same is true for those of us who pray the Liturgy of the Hours. A priest once told me that at times he will see a particular psalm and think to himself, "Oh yes, I know that one," and find himself skipping through it. I told him that I knew what he meant but that I make sure that I pronounce the words rather than just pray the psalms mentally. That's a case, I think, of vocal prayer coming to the aid of mental prayer. Nevertheless, it's difficult to concentrate on what you're saying while praying the psalms. The pope has (rightly) urged those who pray the Liturgy of the Hours to concentrate on what they're praying, but that's often hard to do.

We are not expected to concentrate on some prayers, the most obvious example being the rosary. Although we recite the *Hail Mary* over and over, we are supposed to be thinking about the mysteries. I'm planning to write more about the rosary in a later letter, but I wanted to use it as an example in the context of what we're now discussing. The distractions that come while reciting the rosary don't direct our attention away from the *Hail Mary*s but away from meditating on the mysteries.

Anyway, I'm sure that we are agreed that distractions are a major problem when it comes to all prayer—meditation and contemplation as well as vocal prayer. I may be wrong, but I think the problem is most common when praying ready-made prayers or our own prayers that we've prayed so often that we pray them without thinking about them. I don't think, though, that we should worry too much about distractions, just turn back to our prayers when we become aware of them and realize that God understands that we mean well.

Discursive Meditation

Dear St. Francis,

There is no doubt that you preferred meditation to vocal prayer. In fact, I thought you were somewhat lukewarm in encouraging vocal prayer. You acknowledged that "it is a good thing" to say vocal prayers, but "if you have the gift of mental prayer, you should always give it first place." You went so far as to say, "During vocal prayer if you find your heart drawn and invited to interior or mental prayer, don't refuse to take it up and don't be concerned at not finishing the vocal prayers you intended to say. The mental prayer you substitute for them is more pleasing to God and more profitable for your soul. I make an exception for the Divine Office." (I intend to write about the Divine Office in a later letter.)

It's good that you wrote "if you have the gift of mental prayer" because apparently not everyone has been given that gift. It requires a good bit of attentiveness and that is sometimes difficult to achieve. Fortunately, we Christians have plenty of things to help us: the Bible, spiritual books of all types, paintings or statues, the liturgical texts for the day, the wonders of God's creation, even the events of the day. The thing about meditation is that it can engage our thoughts, imagination, emotions and desires, all in the act of praying.

Did you or did you not, St. Francis, consider meditation a form of prayer? In *Treatise on the Love of God*, you specifically wrote that meditation is only an intermediate exercise leading to prayer. And yet you are famous as one of those who promoted what is known as discursive meditation and today discursive meditation is considered to be prayer. It's a method of prayer that involves three basic steps: thinking of some religious truth, consideration of its application to one's life, and a resolution to put it into practice.

You devoted eight sections of *Introduction to the Devout Life* to meditation, including three sections just on preparations for meditation. I hope you won't mind if I repeat some of what you wrote, so I can comment on those things. I promise not to do that nearly as much in future letters.

The first point of preparation, you wrote,

is to place yourself in the presence of God and invoke his assistance. This seems important no matter how we are to pray. If we're going to have a conversation with God we should place ourselves in his presence.

You wrote paragraphs about four ways to place ourselves in God's presence: (1) a lively, attentive realization of God's absolute presence, that is, that God is in all things and all places; (2) a realization that he is present in a most particular manner in our hearts and in the very center of our spirit; (3) a realization that Jesus in his humanity gazes down from heaven on all people; and (4) the use of our imagination just as we sometimes imagine a friend to be present.

I find it helpful simply to think, "I place myself in your presence, Jesus." This is easiest to do in a church, of course, where Jesus is truly present in the tabernacle, and you, St. Francis, do say that praying is easiest to do in church. However, as you also say, God is everywhere and we can enter into his presence anywhere.

Perhaps too many people skip over your second point of preparation. You advised acknowledgment that we are most unworthy to appear before such sovereign majesty, but since the supreme goodness wills that it should be so, we should implore his grace in order to serve and adore him properly in our meditation. We should ask God for his help in making our meditation, and not only God but the saints and our guardian angel as well.

What you call the third point of preparation, I consider the beginning of the meditation itself. You suggest picturing in imagination the entire mystery we wish to meditate on as if it really took place here before us. This seems to me to be the essence of meditation. We can picture in our minds the scene of the Annunciation, the Crucifixion, the Resurrection or any other scene in the life of Christ. We can put ourselves in the picture and imagine ourselves as careful observers.

I have to say, though, that I was somewhat taken back by the simile you used. You said that using our imagination in this way restricts our mind to the mystery on which we meditate so that it will not wander about, "just as we cage a bird or put a leash on a hawk so he can rest on our hand." I really have never had any desire to have a hawk rest on my hand. I do, though, understand the desirability of keeping our minds from wandering and using our imaginations to picture mysteries.

That's not always possible though. How do we form a picture with our imaginations when meditating about God's will for us or about some of God's awesome attributes—his omniscience, omnipotence, immutability, eternal existence, etc.? In those cases, as you suggest, we need to use some comparisons to assist us.

You then went on to say, "After the imagination has done its part there follows the act of the intellect and this we term meditation." I suppose it's clear from what I said above that I consider the work of the imagination also to be part of meditation. Actually, I think you do, too. Since you called the act of the intellect the second part of meditation, the work of the imagination must be the first part. What you suggest is "to make one or more considerations in order to raise our affections to God and the things of God."

These "considerations" are things that will encourage a greater love of God or an increase in virtue. When meditating on the passion and death of Jesus, for example, it certainly should not be difficult to elicit a reciprocal love for Jesus, who loved us so much that he suffered and died to redeem us. Meditation is meant to produce such sentiments, and you mentioned a number of them: love of God and neighbor, desire for heaven and glory, zeal for the salvation of souls, imitation of the life of our Lord, compassion, awe, joy, fear of God's displeasure, judgment and hell, hatred of sin, confidence in God's goodness and mercy, and deep sorrow for the sins of our past life.

From these sentiments should flow resolutions, which you called the third part of meditation. You pointed out, correctly of course, that we need special practical resolutions in order to correct our faults because affections alone won't do the trick. I'm afraid this is where so many of us slip up. We might find it easy to imagine a scene, consider various aspects of it, and feel compassion, but we're rather slow at the business of making resolutions to correct a fault.

Finally, you wrote, we must conclude our meditation with three acts: an act of thanksgiving to God for the affections and resolutions he has given us, an act of offering to God his own goodness and mercy along with our affections and resolutions, and an act of supplication by which we implore God to bless our affections and resolutions so that we may faithfully fulfill them.

One of the things I found interesting, St. Francis, is that your instructions about prayer, including meditation, are in the second part of *Introduction to the Devout Life*, but in the first part you give detailed instructions on making ten meditations. The ten meditations are on our creation, on the end for which we were created, on God's benefactions, on sin, on death, on judgment, on hell, on paradise, the election and choice of heaven, and the election and choice the soul makes of a devout life. Don't you think it would have been better to tell Philothea how to meditate before presenting those meditations? I'm sorry to be critical here, but that's the way I see it.

Each of those ten meditations follows the instructions you gave in the second part of your *Introduction to the Devout Life*. They begin with preparation, are followed by several consider-ations, then affections and resolutions, and finally the conclusion. I do note, though, that you usually had to skip over what you called the third point of preparation—the use of the imagination to picture a scene. You included that only in the meditations on death and hell. I guess trying to imagine a scene didn't seem appropriate for the other meditations.

May I note, St. Francis, that none of those ten meditations centers on the life and passion of our Lord? And yet you specifically encour-aged meditation on that. I believe that the Church provides one of the best ways to medi-tate on Christ's passion and death. I'm referring to the Stations of the Cross. I try to make the Stations every Friday, in church when possible or by reading a booklet on the Stations if get-ting to church is not possible.

At the end of your instructions about meditation, you added a section on the dryness sometimes experienced while trying to medi-tate. I'm sure I'll address that and other difficul-ties in prayer in a later letter, but my next one will be on contemplative prayer.

Contemplation

Dear St. Francis,

The Church has always taught that there are three expressions of prayer: vocal prayer, meditation, and contemplative prayer. But you seldom mentioned vocal prayer and I don't think you mentioned contemplative prayer at all. I find that somewhat curious unless you thought that contemplative prayer was for those who were advanced in a prayer life and you were simply "introducing" Philothea to the devout life. You yourself were known to spend long hours in front of the Blessed Sacrament and I can only guess that some of that time was spent in contemplation, not wholly in meditation.

I'm going to take the cue from you and not say much about contemplative prayer. I don't feel that I should ignore it, though, because contemplative prayer has always been considered the summit of the Christian life of private prayer. However, it is not for everyone. As Thomas Merton made clear in his book *Contemplative Prayer*, true contemplation "can come to us *only* as a gift, and not as a result of our own clever use of spiritual techniques." The *Catechism of the Catholic Church* agrees, saying, "It is a *gift*, a grace; it can be accepted only in humility and poverty. Contemplative prayer is a *covenant* relationship established by God within our hearts."

By contemplative prayer I mean what is called "the prayer of the heart," the wordless and total surrender of the heart in silence. It's the type of prayer the great mystics prayed, but it's not confined to mystics. It seems most proper to those who have been chosen by God to lead a contemplative life in a monastery, although I acknowledge that more and more lay people are leading contemplative lives in the world. "Centering prayer" is now being taught in many places and those who are interested in it can find books on the subject.

As I understand it, contemplation differs from meditation in that the mind is active in meditation but passive in contemplation. Contemplation is listening in silence, the poor and humble surrender to God and a desire for union with him. It can be either acquired (ascetical contemplation) or infused (mystical contemplation) depending on whether we try to practice it on our own or if it's supernatural in origin.

Thomas Merton warned us against a false contemplation, a quietistic view of contemplative prayer. He wrote that a person cannot become a contemplative merely by "blacking out" sensible realities and remaining alone with himself in darkness. "He is not alone with God, but alone with himself," he wrote. "He is not in the presence of the Transcendent One, but of an idol: his own complacent identity. He becomes immersed and lost in himself, in a state of inert, primitive and infantile narcissism."

Merton continued: "The trouble with quietism is that it cheats itself in its rationalization and manipulation of reality. It makes a cult out of 'sitting still,' as if this in itself had a magic power to solve all problems and bring man into contact with God.… One imagines that by ceasing to be active one automatically enters into contemplation. Actually, this leads one into a mere void." That pretty much sums up my experience.

St. John of the Cross said, in *The Ascent of Mount Carmel*, that we shouldn't even try to practice contemplative prayer until these three signs indicate that we are ready to move on from meditation: (1) One is unable to make discursive meditation as before because of aridity; (2) one has no inclination or desire to fix the mind on anything else; and (3) one desires only to remain alone in loving awareness of God, without any particular knowledge or understanding.

I admit that I have tried centering prayer — sitting in silence and trying to empty my mind in order to unite myself with God. It just doesn't work for me. I guess I haven't been given the gift. However, I can sit back, stop active meditation and ready-made prayers, and think, "Your servant is listening, Lord. I've been talking to you, so now it's time for me to listen to you." Then I keep an active mind so it can "hear" what God wants to say to me, since a conversation should be two-way. I'm convinced that God does indeed speak to me in the silence because I have received ideas about things to write about or things I should be doing that I don't think I would have thought about on my own. There seems to be a difference, though, between listening to what God wants to say and seeking union with him by keep your mind blank.

One of the most popular forms of contemplation is the "Jesus prayer." Since, as the *Catechism* says, "Contemplation is a gaze of faith, fixed on Jesus," the mental repetition of the name "Jesus" is the simplest way of praying. This can take the form that was originally developed by the desert fathers, namely, "Lord Jesus Christ, Son of God, have mercy on me."

It's an invocation that we can repeat throughout the day while we carry on our work, or we can do it in our private room in silence.

The *Catechism* says, "The one name that contains everything is the one that the Son of God received in his incarnation: Jesus.... The name 'Jesus' contains all: God and man and the whole economy of creation and salvation. To pray 'Jesus' is to invoke him and to call him within us." Since the name "Jesus" means "God saves," his name is the only one that contains the presence it signifies.

The *Catechism* also says, "When the holy name is repeated often by a humbly attentive heart, the prayer is not lost by heaping up empty phrases, but holds fast to the word and 'brings forth fruit with patience.' "

I'm not going to write more about contemplation, St. Francis, since you didn't either. Apparently you didn't consider it essential for the devout life and recognized that it is a gift from God. Not all of us are contemplatives.

Liturgical Prayer

Dear St. Francis,

I'd like to turn now, St. Francis, to liturgical prayer. This seems appropriate after that letter about contemplative prayer because, as Thomas Merton said in his book *Contemplative Prayer*, "Liturgy by its very nature tends to prolong itself in individual contemplative prayer, and mental prayer in its turn disposes us for and seeks fulfillment in liturgical worship."

Or perhaps I should have written about liturgical prayer before contemplative prayer since St. Benedict wrote that secret and contemplative prayer should be inspired by liturgical prayer and should be the normal crown of that prayer. Liturgy is the public worship of God and also a participation in Christ's own prayer.

Although there seems to be some debate (especially among members of contemplative religious orders) about whether liturgical or contemplative prayer is best, you had no doubts about the matter. You wrote, "To say it once and for all, there is always more benefit and consolation to be derived from the public offices of the Church than from private particular acts. God has ordained that communion in prayer must always be preferred to every form of private prayer."

There is no doubt, of course, that the Eucharistic Celebration (the Mass) is the summit of liturgical prayer. You, St. Francis, could hardly have been stronger in your words about the liturgical celebration of the Eucharist. You called it "the sum of all spiritual exercises—the most holy, sacred, and supremely sovereign sacrament and sacrifice of the Mass, center of the Christian religion, heart of devotion, and soul of piety, the ineffable mystery that comprises within itself the deepest depths of divine charity, the mystery in which God really gives himself and gloriously communicates his graces and favors to us." If only more people would feel the way you did.

Attendance at weekly Mass has slipped badly during recent decades because some Catholics simply have never learned to appreciate what we have in the Mass. The Eucharist is prayer, of course, but it is more than prayer. It is the source and summit of the Christian life, the sacrament of all sacraments, the memorial of Christ's work of salvation accomplished by his death and resurrection. It is Christ himself who offers the Eucharistic sacrifice and Christ himself, really present in the bread and wine, who is offered. The Church believes that the sacrifice of Christ on the cross and the sacrifice of the Eucharist are one single sacrifice. The celebration of the Eucharist includes thanksgiving and praise to the Father, the sacrificial memorial of Christ and his body, and the presence of Christ by the power of his word and of his Spirit.

You understood all that, of course, St. Francis, which is why you encouraged Philothea to make every effort to assist at Mass every day. I haven't seen statistics on the matter and I could be wrong, but it seems to me that, while the percentage of Catholics who attend Mass on Sunday has definitely declined, the number who attend daily Mass has increased. Wherever I travel in the United States I find daily Masses crowded—where there still are daily Masses, that is, since many parishes no longer can have daily Masses because of a shortage of priests.

Too many people today, though, say that they don't go to Mass because they "don't get anything out of it." Or perhaps it's more along the lines of, "I have a close relationship with

God, pray privately, and try to do good for others. I can be a good Catholic without going to Mass."

I'm not sure how it was in your day, but a strange phenomenon is happening today. While more people claim to be interested in spirituality, the number of those who regularly go to church keeps declining. Spirituality has become a private matter, divorced from the institutional Church. "I can pray in the quiet of my home; I don't have to go to church" has become a common refrain.

Perhaps this comes from the individualism that is often seen as an American virtue. We value individualism so much that we think of spirituality in strictly private terms.

Certainly private devotions, including prayer, periods of meditation, and the reading of Scripture (all the subjects of these letters) are to be encouraged. But one cannot be a true Catholic only privately. Catholicism has always been, and is meant to be, a communal religion.

When Jesus taught his disciples the Lord's Prayer, he prayed "*Our* Father," not "*My* Father," and he asked God to "give *us* our daily bread," "forgive *us* our trespasses," "lead *us* not into temptation," and "deliver *us* from evil." Even when we pray that prayer in private we are uniting ourselves with other Christians.

Prayers directed to Mary, the mother of Jesus, follow that example. In the *Hail Mary*, we ask her to "pray for *us* sinners" and in the *Hail Holy Queen* (*Salve Regina*) plural nouns and pronouns are used throughout.

To understand why it's essential for good Catholics to attend church services, whether or not they "get anything out of it," let's remember what a Catholic community is: It is the people of God gathered around the person of Christ and sharing in his Spirit. The Church is the people. It has Christ as its head, the Holy Spirit as the condition of its unity, the law of love as its rule, and the kingdom of God as its destiny.

All of us need some quiet time alone to develop our individual spirituality, but that must not replace joining others for worship. We humans are essentially social by nature and going to church is what we should do precisely so as not to be alone.

There is a time and a place for private prayers and a time and place for communal prayers. We must stop trying to figure out what we can get out of going to church and concentrate more on what we can contribute by our presence and active participation in worshiping God. The purpose of going to church is to give adoration and praise to God—to give, not to receive. If we do that, we probably will quickly learn that we are also getting more out of going to church.

I'm sorry, St. Francis, if I got carried away there. I shouldn't be preaching to you. I guess it's just something I feel strongly about.

You wrote detailed instructions on how to attend Mass that are as good as anything I've seen on that subject. They also show that, even with changes in the Mass since the seventeenth century, the Mass is essentially the same.

"From the beginning of the Mass until the priest goes up to the altar," you wrote, "make your preparation with him. This consists in placing yourself in the presence of God, recognizing your unworthiness, and asking pardon for your sins." We still have the Penitential Rite during which we do all those things.

"From the time he goes up to the altar until the Gospel consider our Lord's coming and his life in this world by a simple, general consideration." This is fine except that today the priest doesn't actually go to the altar until the offering of the gifts, or what used to be called the Offertory.

"From the Gospel until after the Creed consider our Savior's preaching and affirm that you are resolved to live and die faithful and obedient to his holy word and in union with the holy Catholic Church." For some reason, you didn't mention listening intently to the homily (or the sermon, as it was called in your day). I would think that our resolutions should come directly from the scriptural readings and the words of the homilist.

"From the *Creed* to the *Our Father* apply your heart to the mysteries of the passion and death of our Redeemer." This is the center of the Eucharistic celebration when we should be making the strongest efforts to keep distractions away so we can concentrate on the great Paschal mystery.

I'm surprised that you didn't say anything specifically about the Consecration and Elevation of the Body and Blood of Christ. As the consecrated host is being elevated, I believe it is an opportunity for simple acts of faith, love and adoration: "I believe in you, I love you, and I adore you." At the elevation of the cup, I pray, "My Jesus, mercy. May I be purified by your precious Blood."

You wrote, "From the *Our Father* to Communion strive to excite a thousand desires in your heart and ardently wish to be joined and united forever to our Savior in everlasting love." We should be thinking that we are about to be intimately united with Jesus as we receive his Body and Blood in the form of bread and wine, and what an awesome thing that is!

"From Communion to the end of Mass

give thanks to Jesus Christ for his incarnation, life, passion and death, and for the love he manifests in this Holy Sacrifice." This is the time for our prayers of adoration, praise, thanksgiving, petition, and intercession.

I know this letter is getting somewhat long, but I can't finish writing about the Eucharistic Liturgy without saying something about the way the Mass is celebrated. I know that liturgists are constantly trying to make the Mass more appealing, but I wish they'd stop. Let them concentrate on teaching the younger generations to appreciate the Mass for what it is—as you and I have described it above—and not think that they have to make the Mass more entertaining in order to attract the young people.

I also wish that so many priests didn't think that they have to make the Mass just a bit different. Let them just follow the rubrics. In this regard, C.S. Lewis said it as well as anyone when he was commenting on the liturgies of his Church of England: "The perfect church service would be one we were almost unaware of; our attention would have been on God. But every novelty prevents this. It fixes our attention on the service itself; and thinking about worship is a different thing from worshiping.... A still worse thing may happen. Novelty may fix our attention not even on the service but on the celebrant."

I started this letter writing about liturgical prayer, but all I've written about is the Mass, and there's more than that to liturgical prayer. I'll get to that in a later letter. But first I have more to say about Holy Communion and the sacrament of penance, and I'll do that in my next letter.

Confession and Communion

Dear St. Francis,

Before I continue on the subject of liturgical prayer, I wanted to react to some of the things you wrote about Holy Communion and the sacrament of penance, or confession. You, of course, discussed what you called "holy confession" before Communion because, when you lived, Catholics seldom received Communion without first going to confession. Boy, has that changed!

You instructed Philothea to "make a humble, devout confession every week and always, if possible, before you go to Communion even though you are not conscious of being guilty of mortal sin." Today few people—mainly religious who live in community who probably have fewer sins to confess—receive the sacrament of penance weekly. Those born before Vatican II are generally the only ones who go once or twice a month. More people receive the sacrament once or twice a year, during Lent or during both Lent and Advent. (I hate to admit it, but that's where I fit these days.) But many Catholics these days never receive the sacrament. Gone are the days of my childhood when we were expected to stop at the church on the way home from a Saturday afternoon western at the movie theater in order to go to confession.

It's as if sin no longer exists. Indeed, the younger generations of Catholics do not consider sinful many things that we older people were taught are sins. For example, one need only look at the surveys that show that only a minority of young people considers pre-marital sexual relations to be sinful. I had one young man say to me, "The commandment forbids adultery, and sex on a date between two unmarried people isn't adultery." The number of unmarried couples who live together before marriage has increased to such an extent that it has become acceptable in American society, including among Catholics. There's no thought of sin.

Not being a priest who hears confession, I have no way of knowing the answer to this question, but when was the last time a priest had someone confess that he or she had coveted anything or anyone?

I don't know the solution to the problem

of the decline in the use of the sacrament of penance and reconciliation. I don't think there's a chance that people will avail themselves of the sacrament to the extent they did when you, St. Francis, were alive.

Well, that's enough of that in a letter that's supposed to be focusing on prayer. I included this short comment on the sacrament of penance because you did so in the part of your book about prayer and the sacraments. I'm convinced of the importance of the sacrament and realize that I should take advantage of it more often than I do.

Now I want to react to your comments about frequent Communion. You encouraged it, but with some reservations. You agreed with St. Augustine when you said, "I neither condemn nor unreservedly approve daily Communion.... It would be imprudent to advise everyone indiscriminately to receive Communion frequently, but it would also be imprudent to blame anyone for doing so." You also wrote that a "prudent director" might advise you not to go to Communion so often if others are "disturbed or bothered at seeing you communicate so frequently."

I can report to you, St. Francis, that today nobody would be disturbed or bothered by such a thing. Unlike in your day, frequent Communion is the norm rather than the exception in the Catholic Church today. People usually go to Communion every time they go to Mass. Indeed, the *Catechism* encourages that: "The Church warmly recommends that the faithful receive Holy Communion each time they participate in the celebration of the Eucharist."

The problem today is that people go to Communion so often that it has become routine for some of them. When I serve as extraordinary minister of the Eucharist (I realize that that is a foreign term to you), I see how careless and nonchalant people often are at receiving the Eucharist into their hands, not considering that they are holding and receiving the very Body of Christ. I believe, too, that you might think it a scandal that everybody in the congregation automatically goes up to receive Communion whether or not they might have committed serious sin.

You also touched on another issue that no one in this day and age would even think about. You wrote that "it is improper, although not a grave sin, to solicit payment of the marriage debt on Communion days, but it is not improper but meritorious to pay it. Hence no one ought to be kept from Communion for paying this debt, if otherwise their devotion incites them to seek Communion." Fortunately, the Church has come a long way in its theology of conjugal sanctity and the place of marital sex since your day. You obviously thought there was something at least a bit shady about sexual activity between husband and wife, enough to say that it is improper for one or the other to ask for sexual intercourse before going to Communion.

Fortunately, the attitude toward sexuality that I think you betrayed with that advice no longer exists in the official teachings of the Church today. The *Catechism of the Catholic Church* says plainly, "In marriage the physical intimacy of the spouses becomes a sign and pledge of spiritual communion." We believe today that marital sex is a positive good, not just something reluctantly permitted in order to procreate. Asking a spouse for sex certainly should not be considered improper on Communion days.

If you thought that sexual intercourse between spouses was at least a bit dubious, I'll shock you by what I'm going to say next: The intimacy of receiving Holy Communion can be compared to that of husband and wife in sexual intercourse. In Communion I receive the body of Jesus into my body as a husband and wife become one flesh during intercourse. Nothing could be more intimate. In Communion the divinity of Christ becomes part of my humanity just as I pray that some day I will share in his divinity. It is the closest I can get to Jesus in this life just as sexual intercourse is the closest that husbands and wives can get to one another. I'm sorry, St. Francis, if I shocked you.

Many Catholics want this intimacy with Jesus so much that they receive Communion daily even if they cannot attend Mass. At our parish we have two Communion Services, conducted by laypeople, mainly for those who must get to work early and cannot attend the 8:15 Mass. And with the shortage of priests now, many parishes have daily Communion Services because no priest is available to say Mass.

I realize, though, that there are dangers in this. I know that some people attend a Communion Service when they really could attend Mass if they wanted to, but they go to the Communion Service because it's shorter. The danger is that they fail to appreciate the difference between the Mass and a Communion Service.

My next letter will get back to liturgical prayer, this time focusing on the Liturgy of the Hours.

Liturgy of the Hours

Dear St. Francis,

My letter on liturgical prayer was getting long, so I thought I'd better write a separate one about the Liturgy of the Hours, or the Divine Office.

I agree wholeheartedly with what you wrote to Philothea, namely that "besides hearing Mass on Sundays and holy days, you should assist at the Liturgy of the Hours, especially Vespers, as far as convenience permits. As these days are dedicated to God, we must perform more acts in his honor and glory on them than on other days." The Divine Office is quite appropriate for Sundays and holy days.

I'd go much further than that, though. I'd like to see more members of the laity pray the Liturgy of the Hours every day, not just on Sundays and holy days. Actually, I think that if we could get them to pray the Office on Sundays they would soon start doing so every day. Most

Catholics simply have yet to discover the Liturgy of the Hours. You wrote that St. Augustine, in his *Confessions*, said that at the beginning of his conversion, when he heard the Divine Office his heart melted with happiness and his eyes overflowed with tears of piety. Perhaps modern Catholics wouldn't show quite that much emotion, but I think the Church could interest more members of the laity into saying the Liturgy of the Hours, at least Morning and Evening Prayers, if it tried to do so.

Often, when I say something about the Liturgy of the Hours to lay people, they ask, "What's that?" The Liturgy of the Hours includes prayers—mainly the psalms—for various times of the day—morning, daytime, evening and night. Reciting these prayers is a way to join in the unity of the Church because people throughout the world—mainly priests and religious—are praying the same prayers each day. This is the way the Church follows the apostolic exhortation to "pray always."

The Liturgy of the Hours divides the year up into its liturgical seasons and I find that it's a way of taking all of the great mysteries of the life of Jesus and spreading them out through the whole year. Another part of the Liturgy of the Hours is the Office of Readings. It, too, has psalms, but also readings from both Scripture and from the writings of saints. When it's the feast of some saint, if she or he has written anything, there's an excerpt from that. Or if it's the feast of a martyr, there might be a description of the heroic way that he or she died.

It's true, of course, that the Liturgy of the Hours has historically been recited, or chanted, primarily in monasteries, and most Catholics think of it as something monks and nuns do. But the Second Vatican Council's *Constitution on the Sacred Liturgy* tried to make it clear that it "is intended to become the prayer of the whole People of God." It said that members of the Church "participate according to their own place in the Church and the circumstances of their lives: priests devoted to the pastoral ministry, because they are called to remain diligent in prayer and the service of the word; religious, by the charism of their consecrated lives; all the faithful as much as possible."

That document went on to say, "Pastors of souls should see to it that the principal hours, especially Vespers, are celebrated in common in church on Sundays and on the more solemn feasts. The laity, too, are encouraged to recite the Divine Office, either with the priests, or among themselves, or even individually." I don't know how many churches have Vespers on Sundays and holy days, but I'm sure it's quite rare.

In recommending the introduction of the

Liturgy of the Hours to more laity, I don't for a minute believe that most lay people can pray them as monks and nuns do. And I realize that you would be the first to remind me that "purely contemplative, monastic, and religious devotion cannot be exercised in the homes of married people," as you said in the *Introduction*. Busy mothers with small children would especially find it difficult to find the time. Many people could, though, as those who belong to secular institutes have learned. Each of the "hours" really doesn't take that much time when prayed individually—usually five to ten minutes, or perhaps fifteen minutes for the Office of Readings.

If you look at it one way, those who pray the breviary individually have an advantage over those monks and nuns who pray it in community: We don't have to say it at specific times as they do when they pray it together. We can pray Morning Prayer anytime before noon, Daytime Prayer anytime from mid-morning to mid-afternoon, and Evening Prayer anytime from late afternoon to bedtime. Whenever we pray it, we're joining someone somewhere in the official prayer of the Church.

The Liturgy of the Hours is also an excellent preparation for silent prayer. As the *Catechism* says at one point, "The *lectio divina*, where the Word of God is so read and meditated that it becomes prayer, is thus rooted in the liturgical celebration."

The *Catechism* also calls the Liturgy of the Hours "an extension of the Eucharistic celebration." It complements various other devotions, including and especially adoration and worship of the Blessed Sacrament.

The Church thinks the Liturgy of the Hours is important. If more people would try it, I'm sure they'll find that they like it.

Prayers of Petition

Dear St. Francis,

Certainly not you, St. Francis, but some others who might be reading these letters might wonder how I could write seven letters to you about prayer without discussing prayers of petition. Such prayers are, undoubtedly, the most common—perhaps too common even if the *Catechism* tells us that "when we share in God's saving love, we understand that *every need* can become the object of petition" (emphasis in the *Catechism*).

That may be true, but I can't help but wonder at times. When Notre Dame and Boston College are playing each other in football, and both teams are praying for victory, what's the good Lord to do? And does he really care who wins? I'm all for the players gathering together for prayer before a game to pray that each player will perform to his or her best ability and that there will be no serious injuries, and after a game to give thanks to God, but I question putting him on the spot by praying for victory.

They say that prayers of petition are the lowest and least essential kind of prayer because they are self-centered. But aren't they also the most human? Was Jesus being self-centered or just completely human when, in the Garden of Gethsemane, he prayed, "Take this cup away from me"? Of course, he prefaced that prayer with, "Father, if you are willing," which should be the way we begin all our prayers of petition.

The greatest prayer of petition undoubtedly is for the wisdom to know God's will for us and the courage and ability to do it. I'll have more to say about that in a later letter.

It seems today that the whole concept of prayer is synonymous with petition. "What are you praying for?" As if we are always praying "for" something when we pray. We pray for good health, for success in school or in our profession, for a happy marriage, for all the things we believe we need in life to make us happy. Perhaps such prayers are not as exalted as prayers of adoration, but so what? We are acknowledging our relationship, our dependence, upon God, and asking him confidently for what we want.

Do prayers of petition really do any good though? Are we supposed to believe that God, who is omniscient and knows from all eternity what is going to happen, is going to change his mind as a result of our prayers? Well, no, not exactly. He doesn't have to change his mind because he knows, from all eternity, that we are going to ask him for something and that he will grant it. I guess you could say that God hears, and answers, our prayers before we ever say them.

St. Augustine tackled this problem. He wrote: "Why [God] should ask us to pray, when he knows what we need before we ask him, may perplex us if we do not realize that our Lord and God does not want to know what we want (for he cannot fail to know it) but wants us rather to exercise our desire through our prayers, so that we may be able to receive what he is preparing to give us."

One difference between us humans and God is that we live in time, but God lives in eternity, when there is no such thing as time. For us, what happened yesterday, or just a second ago, is past, and what will happen tomorrow, or the next year, is still in the future. But in eternity, there is no past and future. Everything is simultaneous, in the present. I suppose we could say that for God everything occurs at the same time except that, for God, we really shouldn't use that word "time."

I've always appreciated C.S. Lewis's description of eternity, from his masterpiece *Mere*

Christianity: "If you picture time as a straight line along which we have to travel, then you must picture God as the whole page on which the line is drawn. We come to the parts of the line one by one: we have to leave A behind before we get to B, and cannot reach C until we leave B behind. God, from above or outside or all round, contains the whole line, and sees it all."

This is important if we are to consider the question of human freedom despite the fact that God knows everything that is going to happen. God does not *foresee* us doing something tomorrow or next year anymore than he *saw* us doing something yesterday. He simply *sees* us doing it, whether past, present or future. In God's eternity both yesterday and tomorrow are eternally present. For you and me, yesterday is past and tomorrow hasn't come yet, but that's not true in eternity.

So God doesn't have to change his mind in order to answer our prayers and make something happen in our future that otherwise wouldn't have, because our future is the present for him. Furthermore, his knowledge of what we are going to do in the future doesn't destroy our freedom to decide whether or not we are going to do them. He knows our future actions to be the freely performed actions they are.

Other people have a different objection to

prayers of petition: How, they ask, could God possibly answer the prayers of all those people who are praying to him at the same time? Perhaps they visualize God handling one person's request and then moving on to another's and on down the line until everybody is taken care of. How, they ask, could he have time to handle all those requests?

Of course, that question itself involves "time" and God is not in time. He's in eternity. I suppose we could say that he has all the time he needs except that that answer contains the concept of time. Let's say that he has all eternity in which to listen to all those prayers.

There's still another objection to prayers of petition: Despite Jesus's assurances that all our prayers will be heard, we don't always get what we pray for. Everyone has probably prayed for something and believed that he or she would receive it, and then been disappointed.

My first reaction to that is amazement at the image of God that someone must have who demands that his or her prayer be heard. Is God just a servant waiting to do our bidding? Who's the master and who's the servant here? How dare we ask the awesome God for something and then complain that he didn't hear our prayer or perhaps that he heard it but ignored it!

Perhaps he heard it but knew in his infinite wisdom that what we asked for wouldn't be good for us. He didn't grant our request because of his love for us. He knows far better than we do what we truly need. Or perhaps he didn't grant our request because to do so would mean refusing to answer someone else's prayer, such as those two athletic teams both praying for victory.

Or perhaps he didn't grant our request because it was against his will. If we pray for a big promotion at work and don't get it, maybe that is simply God's will and we should accept it. Remember that Jesus didn't get what he asked for in the Garden of Gethsemane when he prayed that God would take the cup away from him, but he did get the grace to carry out God's will and accomplish his mission of redeeming the world. That's another reason why we must always pray to be able to know what God wants.

In the final analysis, we should pray in faith for what we believe is best for us but be willing to trust in God's greater knowledge of what really is best. We can be sure that, if he doesn't give us exactly what we pray for, he will give us something better.

I wonder, St. Francis, if you were surprised that our *Catechism of the Catholic Church* treats prayers of contrition as part of prayers of petition. I had always considered prayers of contrition as a separate form of prayer, like adoration and thanksgiving. You probably weren't surprised, though, since you stressed that the first thing we must do to live a devout life is to purify the soul, first from mortal sin and then from affection for any sin. You'll be glad to know that our modern *Catechism* quite agrees with you since it says, "The first movement of the prayer of petition is *asking forgiveness*, like the tax collector in the parable: 'God, be merciful to me a sinner!' It is a prerequisite for righteous and pure prayer."

Catholics, of course, learn to pray the Act of Contrition at least by the second grade, the usual time when a child receives the sacrament of penance and reconciliation for the first time. It should be prayed regularly in a healthy spirituality, especially after an examination of conscience at the end of the day.

Other Forms of Prayer

Dear St. Francis,

Since I've written about prayers of petition, let me now turn to prayers of adoration, thanksgiving, intercession and praise.

Of all prayer forms, certainly adoration must rank as the highest. As our *Catechism* tells us, "Adoration is the first attitude of man acknowledging that he is a creature before his Creator. It exalts the greatness of the Lord who made us and the almighty power of the Savior who sets us free from evil."

To some extent every prayer is an act of adoration since we are acknowledging God's greatness and our utter dependence upon him. Whether prayers of blessing, petition, intercession, contrition, or praise, we concede that God is Lord and Master of everything that exists and that all our blessings come from him.

You, St. Francis, had a few things to say about adoration. In your first meditation on our creation you admonished: "Humble yourself profoundly before God, and like the Psalmist say with all your heart: 'Lord, before you I am truly nothing. How were you mindful of me so as to create me?' "

Jesus told us that the greatest commandment is, "You shall love the Lord, your God, with all your heart, with all your soul, and with all your mind." Expressing our love for God by worshiping him is adoration.

The most perfect form of adoration is the Eucharistic Sacrifice because it is the sacrifice that Jesus himself made on the cross as a total offering to God the Father for our salvation. Other forms of worship or adoration, though, are also of great value, especially adoration of Jesus in the Blessed Sacrament. It would be good if more people would make it a practice to get to church in time to adore Jesus in the tabernacle before Mass instead of arriving just when Mass is beginning. When they hurry into the church at the last moment, they are hardly prepared to offer Mass devoutly.

I've mentioned in earlier letters that my parish has a special Adoration Chapel where the consecrated host is exposed in a monstrance every day. Parishioners and non-parishioners have signed up for specific periods of adoration so that someone is in the chapel at all times. This movement of Perpetual Adoration is growing throughout the country and should be encouraged. It's important, though, and difficult to say the least, to make sure that all the hours are covered around the clock throughout the year. Where that isn't possible, especially in small parishes, people should try to get to church regularly (daily if possible) for at least some time of adoration.

Prayers of praise are closest to prayers of adoration because they laud God for his own sake, simply because he is who he is. Many of the psalms are songs of praise. In fact, the title of the collection of the psalms, the Psalter, means "the Praises." I plan to write more about the psalms in a later letter.

The Old Testament Jews didn't praise God only in the psalms, though. Many biblical prayers, and prayers the Jews still say today, begin with, "Blessed are you, our God, King of the universe." God is always called "blessed" because of his great deeds.

St. Paul admonished his readers to praise God by "singing psalms, hymns, and spiritual songs with gratitude in your heart to God." Paul himself gave praise to God frequently in his letters, as he did when he ended his Letter to the Romans with "to the only wise God, through Jesus Christ be glory forever and ever. Amen."

In our liturgy, the doxology—the praise of

God—is the highest moment of expression. The Gloria of the Mass ("Glory to God in the highest") is what is called the Greater Doxology while the prayer "Glory be to the Father, and to the Son, and to the Holy Spirit" is the Lesser Doxology. The Lesser Doxology concludes every psalm and canticle in the Liturgy of the Hours. When Benedictine monks (and perhaps others) chant or recite it, they pay particular reverence by standing and bowing.

The doxology is also appended to the *Our Father*: "For the kingdom, the power and the glory are yours, now and forever."

You, St. Francis, praised God frequently and taught us to do so. Indeed, you concluded the *Introduction to the Devout Life* with praise of God: "Live, Jesus! To whom, with the Father and the Holy Spirit, be all honor and glory, now and throughout the endless ages of eternity. Amen."

Then there are prayers of thanksgiving. Considering all that God has done for us, we should be expressing our gratitude constantly. You urged Philothea to pray prayers of thanksgiving. The third meditation in the *Introduction* is on God's benefactions and you told us, through Philothea, "Thank God for the knowledge he has now given you of your duties and for all benefits already received."

The greatest prayer of thanksgiving, of

course, is the Eucharist. The word itself means thanksgiving, from the Greek *eucharistia*. During the celebration of the Eucharist, time is supposed to be reserved after the reception of Communion for a period of silence for "thanksgiving after Communion." We learned to make this thanksgiving before we received our First Communion, but it seems to me that this period of silence is frequently skipped over in many Masses today. We just want to get on with our hectic lives and if a priest sits too long for meditation after the Communion hymn is over, I can feel people thinking, "Come on, Father, get on with it." If we find a priest who doesn't bow to this pressure, that's one more thing we should thank God for in our prayer of thanksgiving.

Prayers of intercession are nothing more than prayers of petition except that, instead of praying for something for yourself, you pray for someone else. There is no limit to the people we can and should pray for. It even extends to those who have died. I have a long list of people I pray for during my morning devotions—first those who are living and then those who have died.

Is there a Christian parent anywhere who doesn't pray for his or her children? When they leave the nest—even if it's only to go to school —we know that they are beyond our physical care if only for a while, so we ask God (or their guardian angels) to take care of them. Once they leave the nest for good, sometimes the *only* way we can continue to care for them is through our prayers.

We pray for the sick, for those facing a particular trial, for those on a trip, for the newly married, for the bereaved, for those who are having difficulties with their faith, for all of our friends and acquaintances. And yes, we should also pray for our enemies—people that we have antagonized for one reason or another.

Prayers for the dead are a source of controversy because many good Christians believe that it's too late to pray for someone after he or she is dead. In fact, they don't at all understand the Catholic doctrine of purgatory. Neither, though, do many Catholics. For example, they sometimes think of it as a place between heaven and hell, and it is not. Purgatory is the name given to a process of purification, not to a place the soul might go to after death.

Unfortunately, some pious folklore has made purgatory seem like a mini-hell where people spend years and years of torture and pain before finally being allowed into heaven. That, though, is not Catholic teaching. As Pope John Paul II said August 4, 1999, "Those who live in this state of purification after death are not separated from God but are immersed in the love of Christ."

Catholics believe that we, the relatives and friends of the deceased, can assist those who have died with our prayers of intercession. This is part of the doctrine of the communion of saints that we say we believe in when we recite the Apostles' Creed. The souls in purgatory are not separated from the saints in heaven or from us on earth. We all remain united in the Mystical Body of Christ and we can therefore offer up prayers and good works on behalf of our brothers and sisters in their process of purification.

Belief in the efficacy of prayers for the dead goes back at least as far as the Second Book of Maccabees (12:39-46). After Judas had won a battle he found that dead Jewish soldiers had committed a sin by wearing idolatrous amulets under their tunics. He and his men "prayed that the sinful deed might be fully blotted out." Then they took up a collection that he sent to Jerusalem for an expiatory sacrifice. "Thus he made atonement for the dead that they might be freed from this sin," the chapter concludes.

The Catholic Church has always offered prayers for the dead, especially the Eucharistic sacrifice, the most perfect prayer of intercession.

When to Pray

Dear St. Francis,

In the second part of your *Introduction to the Devout Life*, about prayer, you included two sections about prayer at specific times of the day, namely, the morning exercise and the evening exercise and examination of conscience.

It's probably obvious that each individual must decide for himself or herself when the best time of the day for prayer is. In this regard, as in so many others, it depends upon the circumstances. Perhaps for most people, early morning is a good time, but that probably isn't true for young parents busy with getting their children fed and ready for school. For them, perhaps another time is better. Nevertheless, I do know parents who get up early enough in the mornings to pray before the children get up. More power to them.

For me, in my present circumstances, the best times for prayer are precisely those that you suggest—especially since you define evening as "a little before the hour for supper" rather than the time after supper—or for most modern Americans, dinner. (As I was growing up, we had breakfast, dinner and supper, as you obviously did, but today it's breakfast, lunch and dinner.)

You defined morning prayer as "a general preparation for all the day's actions," and you gave four very specific ways to do that. I don't do it quite the way you suggested but I think I follow your instructions generally. I start with something that I think everyone can do, and I do it before I even get out of bed. That is simply to say, "Good morning, Jesus. Everything I do today will be for you." Then I recite the more formal Morning Offering, offering Jesus all my prayers, works, joys and sufferings of the day. During my shower, I continue with a whole string of prayers that I've learned through the years. The problem is, I've been reciting them for so long that they've become routine and I have trouble concentrating on what I'm praying. Although I have the intention to pray, I fear that I am not really lifting up my mind to God.

It's later in the morning, after I've prayed the morning breviary and the rosary and during my period of meditation in church, that I do what you suggest. That's when I, in your words, "anticipate what tasks, transactions, and occasions for serving God you may meet on this day and to what temptations of offending him you will be exposed, whether by anger, vanity, or some other irregularity." In the presence of Jesus, I plan my day and, again in your words, "acknowledge that by [myself I] can do none of the things [I] have decided on, whether of avoiding evil or of doing good."

I'm not suggesting that this is a routine that everyone should follow to improve his or her prayer life. I'm just saying that it usually works for me in the present circumstances of my life. It would not have worked when I was younger and still today there are many days when I don't get to church in the morning and never get in my meditation and planning my day in God's presence. I repeat what I've already said, that everyone must do what experience proves is best for him or her.

The same is true in late afternoon. I find this a good time to say Evening Prayer (or Vespers if we want to retain the Latin term) and the Office of Readings. Some people say the Office of Readings late at night, but the only time I've done that is when I could find no other opportunity during the day. I generally agree with C.S. Lewis that "no one in his senses, if he has any power of ordering his own day, would reserve his chief prayers for bedtime—obviously the worst possible hour for any action which needs concentration. The trouble is that thousands of unfortunate people can hardly find any other."

Prayer before bedtime, though, is important, and good parents have always used bedtime to help their children learn to pray. Perhaps they didn't exist in your time, St. Francis, but today there are many cartoons in our periodicals that show a child kneeling by his bed, saying a prayer that grown-ups consider funny. Bedtime prayer is a good habit to get into, and for us adults it should include an examination of conscience.

I'm sure you agree since you wrote that "the examination of conscience must always be made before going to bed" and you advised that this is where we are to "reflect on where, with whom, and in what work we have been engaged."

I suppose I shouldn't be quoting your words back to you, but you described exactly what bedtime prayers should include in addition to the examination of conscience. You wrote, "After this we recommend to God's providence our body and soul, the Church, our relatives, and friends. We beg our Lady, our guardian angel, and the saints to watch over us and for us. Thus with God's blessing we go to take the rest that he has decreed as necessary for us." Isn't that basically what parents do with their children when they are teaching them to say bedtime prayers?

But, of course, we can pray at other times of the day besides morning, evening and bedtime. Sometime during the day—between Morning Prayer and Evening Prayer—I can usually fit in Daytime Prayer, usually just before lunch. It takes only five minutes. There are times, though, especially when I'm traveling, when the activities of the day simply don't permit me to sit down with the breviary between morning and evening.

That doesn't mean, though, that I can't pray. That's where the "aspirations, ejaculatory prayers, and good thoughts" that you wrote about come in. As you said, ejaculatory prayers "may be interspersed among all our tasks and duties without any inconvenience." I read a book a few years ago in which various people described how they pray. Many of them wrote that they have formed the habit of saying short ejaculations when something occurs during the day. For some reason it sticks in my mind that a well-known archbishop once said that he says a quick prayer when he opens the refrigerator door. He also said that he finds commercial breaks during basketball games on television a good time to pray and that, at the end of close games when there are a lot of time-outs, he could "pray up a storm." He mentioned a friend who prays whenever he pushes the button that opens the garage door.

After reading that, I formed the habit of breathing a quick "Come, Holy Spirit" when I'm getting ready to answer the telephone, asking the Holy Spirit to help me with whatever the caller is calling about.

All of this goes along with what St. John Chrysostom wrote: "It is possible to offer fervent prayer even while walking in public or strolling alone, or seated in your shop, ... while buying or selling, ... or even while cooking."

I know people who pray the rosary while they're driving in a car, either alone or with a spouse, and I admit that I sometimes do that myself. That bothers me, though, because I don't think someone can say the rosary properly and still concentrate on his or her driving. For those who can, more power to them. I'm just saying that it's hard for me and I'm sure that those who do it concentrate on their prayers at least as well as I do when I'm saying morning prayers. By the way, I plan to write more about praying the rosary in a future letter.

Another of your suggestions, St. Francis, is "to retire at various times into the solitude of your own heart even while outwardly engaged in discussions or transactions with others."

Wow! How does one do that? I can understand pausing in the midst of a busy day to say a quick prayer, but to do so *while* outwardly engaged in discussions or transactions? I can't do that. Indeed, I wonder if you really meant that. I'm inclined to think that this sentence is more in line with what you were teaching Philothea: "Our tasks are seldom so important as to keep us from withdrawing our hearts from time to time in order to retire into this divine solitude." That I'll go along with.

I particularly liked your example of St. Catherine of Siena who, when her parents deprived her of all opportunity for time and place to pray, "built a little oratory within her soul where she could retire mentally and enjoy this holy heartfelt solitude while going about her outward duties." Of course, St. Thérèse of Lisieux and many other saints did the same thing. I'm sure that it made the day's duties go much smoother, too.

In the end, of course, it gets back to St. Paul's admonition to "pray always." We must learn how to do everything in the presence of God. It's not easy but it can be done if we frequently remind ourselves that, at the beginning of the day, we have offered all our prayers, works, joys and sufferings to God.

As Origen wrote: "He 'prays without ceasing' who unites prayer to works and good works to prayer. Only in this way can we consider as realizable the principle of praying without ceasing."

Prayers and Posture

Dear St. Francis,

This letter will be short, St. Francis, because I'm in a bit of a hurry. Also, I think it will become apparent that I think it's the least important of this series of letters I'm writing to you. But I'm curious: Did you kneel, stand or sit when you said your prayers? Or did you do all three at various times? Or didn't you consider posture while praying very important?

I don't think I would have brought it up except that it seems to be important to some people. Whether the congregation should kneel or stand during the Eucharistic Prayer during Mass seems to really bother a lot of people. And apparently some people have the idea that kneeling is the "approved" position for praying.

Even C.S. Lewis favored kneeling. He wrote to Malcolm: "When one prays in strange places and at strange times one can't kneel, to be sure. I won't say this doesn't matter. The body ought to pray as well as the soul. Body and soul are both the better for it." Then he went off into a digression before picking up his thought again: "The relevant point is that kneeling does matter, but other things matter even more. A concentrated mind and a sitting body make for better prayer than a kneeling body and a mind half asleep. Sometimes these are the only alternatives."

Well, this time I disagree with half of what Lewis wrote. I don't think that kneeling does matter but I agree that other things matter more and that a concentrated mind is more important. I don't think we should quibble about bodily postures.

Obviously some people can concentrate better while kneeling. We know that Pope John Paul II kneels while praying with tremendous concentration. Many of the mystic saints knelt and were sometimes elevated from the ground while they were praying. A woman who prays regularly in the Adoration Chapel at my parish church kneels motionless for great periods of time. It was said of St. Rose-Philippine Duchesne, who spent a year working among the American Indians, that Indian children would sneak up behind her as she knelt in prayer and sprinkle bits of paper on her habit. When they came back hours later, they found them undisturbed.

That's great. But I refuse to think that one must kneel in order to pray devoutly. If you're going to concentrate your mind on prayer, I think that you have to be in a comfortable position. When I'm uncomfortable I think too much about my discomfort, and I get uncomfortable after kneeling for any length of time. Particularly when I'm meditating, I sit with my eyes closed. Admittedly, that can be carried to extreme if you get so comfortable with your eyes closed that you fall asleep, but normally I can concentrate my mind better when I'm sitting than I can when I'm kneeling. I do most of my kneeling during Mass and while saying private prayers of adoration or contrition. It does seem appropriate to kneel for those prayers.

I think, St. Francis, that you agree with me on this point because you told Philothea that it is neither necessary nor expedient to perform all her devotions on her knees. You told her she could do it while walking outside or even in bed. I was glad to see that advice because I do sometimes say a rosary during my early morning walk, and sometimes I say it in bed.

On a related topic, it's interesting to me the way the practice of holding hands during the *Our Father* at Mass has become a common practice. With no directives from liturgists that I know of, the practice has become widespread across the country. People recognize the practice as a symbol of unity while praying the prayer Jesus taught to us. The official Church has never approved or disapproved the practice but I can't imagine why it would disapprove.

Some of those not holding hands with their neighbors prefer the *orante* position. This is the classical attitude of prayer, standing with one's hands lifted up, with palms facing outward. This posture is meant to convey the idea that, just as his hands are raised, so is the *orante*'s mind and heart raised to God. I've adopted that position during the *Our Father* at Mass unless a neighbor offers his or her hand.

That's really all I wanted to say about prayers and posture, St. Francis. I'll write a longer letter the next time.

The Lord's Prayer

Dear St. Francis,

In your instructions about prayer, St. Francis, you said that we must always conclude our meditations with the *Our Father* and the *Hail Mary*, which you called "the general and necessary prayers of all the faithful." In another place, you advised Philothea to "say your *Pater, Ave Maria,* and *Credo* in Latin, but you should also learn to understand well the words in your own language so that, while saying them in the common language of the Church, you can also appreciate the wonderful and beautiful meaning of those holy prayers."

I guess I needn't tell you that most Catholics today no longer know those prayers in Latin. You can generally tell that someone grew up prior to the Second Vatican Council if he or she can still pray them in Latin—as most of us who memorized them as children can still do. It's like altar boys from that era still being able to recite the *Suscipiat*.

But I digress. The main point you were making was that those prayers "must be said with strict attention of mind and with affections aroused by the meaning of the words. Do not hurry along and say many things but try to speak from your heart. A single *Our Father* said with feeling has greater value than many said quickly and hurriedly."

I grant you that. Unfortunately, as I said in an earlier letter, I have trouble concentrating on ready-made prayers. I have to confess that I recite the *Our Father* without "strict attention of mind" more often than I concentrate on the words. We say the *Our Father* frequently. I figure that I recite it at least nine times a day— the Liturgy of the Hours' morning and evening prayers, six times while saying the rosary, and during Mass. I really must learn to say it with more attention than I usually do.

While you, St. Francis, called the *Our Father* one of the general and necessary prayers, the *Catechism of the Catholic Church* calls it "the fundamental Christian prayer." Some of the Doctors of the Church have had even more powerful words to say about it. St. Thomas Aquinas, for example, called it "the most perfect of prayers" because "in it we ask, not only for all the things we can rightly desire, but also in the sequence that they should be desired.

This prayer not only teaches us to ask for things, but also in what order we should desire them."

St. Augustine wrote: "Run through all the words of the holy prayers [in Scripture], and I do not think that you will find anything in them that is not contained and included in the Lord's Prayer."

It is called the Lord's Prayer, of course, because Jesus himself taught it to us, so we shouldn't be surprised that it is considered the perfect prayer. When he taught it to his disciples, it was new. The Jews, of course, never called God "Father," much less "our Father." It was Jesus, who was God the Son, who not only revealed the Father to us but also taught us that we could have an intimate relationship to him, as we do (hopefully) to our human father. Furthermore, when we pray to the Father we also adore and glorify God the Son and the Holy Spirit since the Trinity is consubstantial and indivisible.

When we pray "who art in heaven," we are not referring to a place off in the distance somewhere but to God's majesty. As St. Augustine wrote, "'Our Father who art in heaven' is rightly understood to mean that God is in the hearts of the just, as in his holy temple." And the *Catechism* says, "When the Church prays 'our Father who art in heaven,' she is professing that we are the People of God, already seated 'with him in the heavenly places in Christ Jesus.'"

The *Catechism* also tells us that, after addressing God and thereby placing ourselves in his presence (as you, St. Francis, told us we must always do as we begin our prayers), we pray seven petitions. "The first three," it says, "more theological, draw us toward the glory of the Father; the last four, as ways toward him, commend our wretchedness to his grace."

This first of the three theological "petitions" don't seem like petitions to me. "Hallowed be thy name" seems more like a prayer of praise. We are praising God for his holiness, recognizing that his name is holy. The *Catechism* teaches us, though, that "this petition is here taught to us by Jesus as an optative: a petition, a desire, and an expectation in which God and man are involved." We are asking, in effect, that the name of God should be made holy in us through our actions. St. Peter Chrysologus, one of the Doctors of the Church, reminded us that "God's name is blessed when we live well, but is blasphemed when we live wickedly."

We then pray, "Thy kingdom come." Although the Kingdom of God has been coming since the Last Supper and is in our midst in the Eucharist, this petition refers primarily to the final coming of the reign of God after Christ's return.

It has always seemed to me that the next petition—"Thy will be done on earth as it is in heaven"—is the heart of the *Our Father*. I understand that some people look on this petition as just one of submission to God's will. I think that submission is included in the petition, but I've always put a lot more into it. When we pray, "Thy will be done" we are praying that we will have the courage to do God's will. It's an active petition, not a passive one. Not only are we to passively suffer whatever God's will is for us, but we are to actively do it.

I don't think anyone has difficulty understanding the next petition: "Give us this day our daily bread." Everyone realizes that "bread" stands for all the things we need—our food and all appropriate things we need, both material and spiritual. We should note, though, that this petition for material needs is the fourth of the seven petitions, not the first. Remember what St. Thomas Aquinas said? "This prayer not only teaches us to ask for things, but also in what order we should desire them."

Now we come to an important petition: "And forgive us our trespasses as we forgive those who trespass against us." It's easy to ask for forgiveness, but Jesus is telling us implicitly that our petition won't be heard unless we first meet a strict requirement, that of forgiving others. Our forgiveness must come first.

I said in the previous paragraph that it's an important petition. Jesus obviously considered it important because it's the only petition to which he returned after teaching the prayer during the Sermon on the Mount. He explained, "If you forgive others their transgressions, your heavenly Father will forgive you. But if you do not forgive others, neither will your Father forgive your transgressions."

The petition "lead us not into temptation" bothers some people. "Why," they ask, "would God 'lead' us into temptation?" Since the Greek verb really means "do not let us yield to temptation," there have been occasional attempts to change the prayer. But the idea of changing the *Our Father* always meets with opposition. Nonetheless, that's what this petition means. We are asking God to keep us from falling into sin. Of course, to do that we have to do our part by avoiding, whenever possible, the things that lead to temptation.

I wonder how many people understand that in the petition "but deliver us from evil," evil is not just an abstraction. It refers to a person, Satan, the Evil One, the devil. There are many people in our society today who say they don't believe in the devil. They're fooling themselves. We need God's continual help to be delivered from him. However, the petition is also a plea to the Father to deliver us from all the distress that exists in this world, of which the Evil One is the instigator.

Early in Christian history, liturgical use of the *Our Father* concluded with a doxology, "For the kingdom, the power and the glory are yours, now and forever." It was not part of the prayer as Jesus taught it. Today the doxology seems to be recited more by Protestants than by Catholics and I admit that I don't use it. It's included in the Catholic liturgy but separated from the main body of the *Our Father* by another prayer. The doxology, of course, allows us to finish the prayer by acknowledging God's titles of kingship, power and glory.

Hail Mary and the Rosary

Dear St. Francis,

In your *Introduction to the Devout Life*, St. Francis, you frequently invoked Mary—the Mother of God, called both the Blessed Virgin and Blessed Mother—but nowhere any more than in this passage: "Honor, reverence, and respect with a special love the sacred and glorious Virgin Mary. She is the mother of our sovereign Lord and consequently she is our own mother in an especial way. Let us run to her and like little children cast ourselves into her arms with perfect confidence. At every moment and on every occasion let us call on this dear mother. Let us invoke her maternal love and by trying to imitate her virtues let us have true filial affection for her."

Before writing about prayers to Mary, perhaps I should say something about Catholics' devotion to her. Many people, Catholics as well as non-Catholics, are troubled by the amount of attention focused on Mary. They believe that it detracts from devotion to Jesus. They believe, in fact, that it at least borders on idolatry. Uninformed people believe that Catholics worship Mary—which *would* be idolatry.

Even some well-informed people, who understand that Catholics do not worship Mary, still believe that our Church honors her too much. When asked why he didn't become a Catholic since it seemed that most of his friends were Catholic, C.S. Lewis replied that he couldn't agree with two aspects of Catholicism: the place given to Mary and the doctrine of papal infallibility.

But just exactly how much attention should rightly be focused on Mary? Some of the people who criticize Catholics for honoring her too much don't seem to honor her at all. And these frequently are good Bible-believing Christians. Mary herself says in her Magnificat, "From now on all generations will call me blessed." Why don't all Christians who believe that the Bible is the inspired word of God call Mary blessed?

It is indeed possible to have an improper devotion to Mary. That happens when the devotion does, in fact, detract from devotion to Jesus. Correct devotion to Mary must always lead to Jesus, not away from him.

Those who pray to Mary for favors "because God won't grant them" have a strange idea of Mary's role. That role is inseparable from Mary's union with Christ. As the *Catechism of the Catholic Church* says, "What the Catholic faith believes about Mary is based on what it believes about Christ, and what it teaches about Mary illumines in turn its faith in Christ."

Bible Christians should particularly be attracted to the Catholic Church's prayer to Mary, the *Hail Mary*, because the first part of the prayer is taken directly from the Bible—the first chapter of Luke's Gospel to be specific. "Hail, Mary, full of grace, the Lord is with thee" were the words of the archangel Gabriel when he appeared to ask Mary to be the mother of God. "Blessed art thou among women and blessed is the fruit of thy womb, Jesus" are the words of Elizabeth when Mary visited her.

In the second half of the prayer, we pray, "Holy Mary, mother of God, pray for us sinners now and at the hour of our death." We confess our faith that Mary is indeed the mother of God because Jesus is God and she is his mother. Since Jesus is only one person, with both a human and a divine nature, Mary is the mother of that one person. It's a belief that Christians have always had and which the Council of Ephesus defined in 431.

The prayer asks Mary to pray for us, to intercede with God for us. Catholics believe that all the saints in heaven can pray for us; it is belief in the communion of saints that Christians say they believe when they recite the *Apostles' Creed*. Mary, as the mother of God, is honored as the greatest of saints so it is natural that we would ask for her intercession.

Mary appears often in the Bible—from the Annunciation and the infancy narratives, through her sorrows as she stood under the cross, to her prayers with the apostles in the Upper Room at the time of Pentecost. Her final words recorded in the Scriptures, though, occur during the wedding feast of Cana: Referring to Jesus, she said, "Do whatever he tells you." That is still what Mary is telling us twenty-first-century Christians.

That brings us to the rosary. The entire rosary includes 150 *Hail Mary*s, divided into fifteen decades with an *Our Father* between each decade, but the rosary most of us are familiar with is only one-third of the entire rosary. The rosary developed in about the twelfth century. At first peasants around a monastery would recite 150 *Our Father*s while the monks in the monastery sang the 150 psalms. Then the practice arose of praying *Hail Mary*s instead of *Our Father*s. When the three groups of mysteries were attached, one-third of the complete rosary was said at one time—fifty *Hail Marys*—the common practice today.

St. Francis, you wrote, "The rosary is a very useful form of prayer provided you know how to say it properly." It is not easy to say the rosary if one is to do it properly. The purpose of the rosary is to help us meditate on the mysteries of our salvation, on the events in the lives of Jesus and Mary. Although the prayer said most often with the rosary is the *Hail Mary*, addressed to Jesus's mother, the main focus is on the birth, life, death and resurrection of Jesus. These are the "mysteries" or events that the pray-er thinks about while praying the rosary.

The rosary has been called the perfect Christian prayer because it combines prayer, meditation and Scripture. The repetition of prayers is meant to create an atmosphere in which to meditate on the mysteries of our salvation as revealed in Scripture. Pope Paul VI said, "By its nature the recitation of the rosary calls for a quiet rhythm and a lingering pace, helping the individual to meditate on the mysteries of the Lord's life as grasped by the heart of her who was closer to the Lord than all others."

The meditations are usually divided into three groups, the joyful, sorrowful and glorious mysteries of our salvation. The joyful mysteries, all taken from Scripture, are the appearance of the archangel Gabriel to Mary to ask her to be Jesus's mother, Mary's visitation to her cousin Elizabeth, the birth of Jesus in Bethlehem, the presentation of Jesus in the temple, and the finding of Jesus in the temple when he was twelve years old.

The sorrowful mysteries are Jesus's agony in the garden, his scourging by the Roman soldiers, the crowning with thorns, the carrying of the cross, and his crucifixion and death on the cross.

The glorious mysteries are Jesus's resurrection from the dead, his ascension into heaven, the descent of the Holy Spirit on the apostles, the assumption of Mary into heaven, and her coronation as queen of heaven and earth. The last two mysteries are not scriptural but are part of the Catholic tradition.

Besides the joyful, sorrowful and glorious mysteries, some people meditate on other events in the life of Christ. Other common mysteries are the salvation, healing, eucharistic and consoling mysteries. Because of the emphasis on meditating on the life of Christ, Pope Pius XII once called the rosary a compendium of the gospel.

A priest from my parish, who has since died, recognized the difficulty of meditating while praying the rosary without distractions.

He told people to think of one word for each of the mysteries and to return to that word if distractions come. I've tried it and it works.

Another way to overcome distractions is by saying the Scriptural Rosary, with a Scripture reading for each *Hail Mary*. Besides meditations for the usual joyful, sorrowful and glorious mysteries, there is also the Seven-Day Scriptural Rosary, with different mysteries for each day of the week.

The rosary has been a popular devotion through the centuries. It's a devotion that honors Mary but, as all true devotion to Mary must do, it leads us to her Son.

In my parish, the rosary is recited aloud every day. However, I don't participate in this prayer. It's just a personal thing with me, but I find that I don't meditate on the mysteries nearly as well when I'm praying the rosary in a group as I do when I'm praying it by myself. I consider the rosary a private, rather than a communal, devotion. Obviously, others feel differently about that.

The *Hail Mary* and the rosary, though, are not the only prayers that Catholics direct to Mary. I'll discuss some of the other prayers in my next letter.

Other Prayers to Mary

Dear St. Francis,

I have to tell you, St. Francis, that I was a bit disappointed that your *Introduction to the Devout Life* didn't say more about devotion to Mary than it did, since that devotion is so integral to the beliefs of the Catholic Church. And when it came to prayers to the Virgin, the only ones you mentioned were the *Hail Mary* and the rosary. I'm quite certain that you yourself prayed several other prayers to the Blessed Virgin. Let me briefly write about some of them that you could have included.

First there's the *Salve Regina.* (Since you like to call prayers by their Latin names I'll do so, too). Today this prayer is still often sung in Latin in some places. It originated in the eleventh century at the famous shrine to Mary at Le Puy en Velay, in southeastern France, not too far from where you lived in Switzerland. This was the time when devotion to Mary was most pronounced, nowhere more than in France. There was an old statue of the Virgin and Child, of unknown origin, in the little church at Le Puy, and miracles were attributed to prayers in front of that statue to Mary for her intercession.

Le Puy was on the route traveled by pilgrims going to the famous shrine of St. James at Compostela in Spain. During the Middle Ages more pilgrims went there than any other place except to Rome and Jerusalem. They found shelter at Le Puy and begged Mary for her guidance and care as they continued their journey.

The prayer goes like this (in English, not in Latin): "Hail, Holy Queen, mother of mercy, our life, our sweetness and our hope! To you do we cry, poor banished children of Eve. To you do we send up our sighs, mourning and weeping in this valley of tears. Turn then, most gracious advocate, your eyes of mercy toward us, and after this our exile show unto us the blessed fruit of your womb, Jesus. O clement, O loving, O sweet Virgin Mary!"

Today the *Salve Regina* is frequently said at the end of the rosary, especially when a group recites the rosary. I don't do that, though, because I've gotten into the habit of reciting the *Salve Regina* as part of my morning prayers as I'm getting ready for the day. Therefore, I prefer to say a different prayer after I finish the rosary.

The prayer I say at the end of the rosary is the *Memorare* (again a Latin name). It goes like this: "Remember, O most gracious Virgin Mary, that never was it known that anyone who fled to your protection, implored your help, or sought your intercession was left unaided. Inspired by this confidence, I fly to you, O Virgin of virgins, my mother! To you I come, before you I stand, sinful and sorrowful. O mother of the Word Incarnate, despise not my petitions, but in your mercy hear and answer me. Amen."

This prayer, imploring Mary's protection, serves as a good night prayer, but I think it's a better prayer for travelers than the *Salve Regina*. If the prayer existed when the shrine at Le Puy was popular, the *Memorare* would have seemed the more popular prayer. As a matter of fact, it might have existed then because the prayer is attributed to St. Bernard of Clairvaux, who lived in the twelfth century. It seems doubtful, though, that he was the real author. The earliest records of its existence date from the fifteenth century and it was made popular only in the seventeenth century, by a French priest named Claude Bernard.

The difference between the *Salve Regina* and the *Memorare* is that the former seems to put Mary on a pedestal, honoring her as a queen, while the latter salutes her as our "gracious" Virgin Mary and calls her "my mother." Perhaps it's just I, but it seems that the *Memorare* somehow seems more intimate, especially since we admit our sinfulness and express sorrow for our sins. Of course, it's true that the *Salve Regina* calls Mary "gracious advocate" and "clement, loving and sweet." Anyway, I recite both prayers daily.

One saint, a Doctor of the Church, who seemed to prefer the *Salve Regina* was Alphonsus Liguori. He wrote an entire book called *The Glories of Mary* that was an explanation of the *Salve Regina.*

Let me next mention the *Magnificat.* The Church considers it so important that it includes it in Vespers (or Evening Prayer) every day. This prayer, of course, isn't to Mary; it's the prayer that Mary herself recited during the Visitation: "My soul proclaims the greatness of the Lord, my spirit rejoices in God my Savior for he has looked with favor on his lowly servant. From this day all generations will call me blessed: the Almighty has done great things for me, and holy is his name. He has mercy on those who fear him in every generation. He has shown the strength of his arm, he has scattered the proud in their conceit. He has cast down the mighty from their thrones, and has lifted up the lowly. He has filled the hungry with good things, and the rich he has sent empty away. He has come to the help of his servant Israel for he has remembered his promise of mercy, the promise he made to our fathers, to Abraham and his children forever."

The Church recommends that those who recite the Liturgy of the Hours say a prayer in honor of the Blessed Virgin at the end of Compline, or Night Prayer. Since I've said other prayers to Mary earlier in the day, I usually select this one: "Loving mother of the Redeemer, gate of heaven, star of the sea, assist your people who have fallen yet strive to rise again. To the wonderment of nature you bore your Creator, yet remained a virgin after as before. You who received Gabriel's joyful greeting, have pity on us poor sinners."

That prayer isn't as well known as other prayers to Mary. It too asks her for her assistance while acknowledging that we "poor sinners" "have fallen." It also expresses faith in one of the doctrines about Mary, her perpetual virginity.

The *Angelus* is considered a Marian prayer (although it really is a declaration of faith in the Incarnation) because three *Hail Mary*s are said between verses and it includes a prayer to the mother of God. This is the prayer that the Church encourages us to recite three times a day and it used to be that church bells rang at 6 a.m., noon, and 6 p.m. to remind us to do so. I still say the prayer three times a day, but not at those particular times. Rather I add them to my morning, daytime, and evening prayers when I'm praying the Liturgy of the Hours. The *Angelus* is an excellent example of the way devotion to Mary leads to Jesus.

The *Angelus* goes like this: "The angel of the Lord declared to Mary and she conceived of the Holy Spirit. (Hail Mary.) Behold the handmaid of the Lord. Let it be done to me according to your will. (Hail Mary.) The Word was made flesh and dwelt among us. (Hail Mary.) Pray for us, O holy mother of God, that we may be made worthy of the promises of Christ.

"Let us pray: Pour forth, we beseech you, O Lord, your grace into our hearts, that we, to whom the Incarnation of Christ your Son was made known by the message of an angel, may by his passion and cross be brought to the glory of his resurrection. Through Christ our Lord. Amen."

During the Easter season, the Church recommends another prayer to Mary: the *Regina Coeli*: "Queen of heaven, rejoice, alleluia. The Son whom you merited to bear, alleluia, has risen as he said, alleluia. Rejoice and be glad,

O Virgin Mary, alleluia! For the Lord has truly risen, alleluia!"

This prayer is used both at the end of Compline in the Liturgy of the Hours and in place of the *Angelus* during the day. When it replaces the *Angelus* this prayer is added: "Let us pray. O God, Who by the resurrection of your Son, Our Lord Jesus Christ, granted joy to the whole world: grant, we beseech you, that through the intercession of the Virgin Mary, his mother, we may lay hold of the joys of eternal life. Through the same Christ our Lord. Amen."

This prayer also seems to date from the twelfth century. Alas, it doesn't seem to be prayed by as many people today as during the period of intense devotion to Mary that existed when it originated.

These, then, are some of the traditional Marian prayers that have come down to us through the centuries. There are, of course, a great many others that can be found in Catholic prayer books, but I think the ones I've included in this letter are probably the most important.

Prayers to the Saints

Dear St. Francis,

You, St. Francis, had a great devotion to other saints besides the Blessed Virgin, as evidenced by the numerous times you mentioned them in your *Introduction to the Devout Life*. Indeed, you had a whole section called "Our Duty to Honor and Invoke the Saints."

In the section where you taught that it was "an error, or rather a heresy, to wish to banish the devout life from" ordinary life, you have a list of saints and others who lived devout lives in the work place. But you obviously had some favorites since you wrote about both "the great St. Louis" and St. Bernard in seventeen places and St. Catherine of Siena in eleven places. (St. Louis, by the way, was one of the saints I included in my book *Married Saints*.)

One of the ways the Catholic Church differs from other religions is in its devotion to saints. It has honored people who lived heroically holy lives since the beginning of Christianity when it began to venerate St. Stephen as the first martyr. For centuries local churches remembered holy people after their deaths, calling them saints and praying to them to ask for their intercession with God. Finally, the popes reserved for themselves the right to declare someone a saint.

The Catholic Church canonizes people not only to honor them—they couldn't care less, being in heaven—but, more important, to offer them as role models. Those of us who are still trying to work out our salvation can try to emulate some of the virtues displayed by those who were so close to God that they were recognized for their holiness. That, of course, is what you, St. Francis, recommended to Philothea.

One of the things some people object to regarding Catholics' devotion to the saints is the idea of praying for their intercession. That practice comes from the doctrine of the communion of saints that is part of the Apostles' Creed. Catholics believe that the saints in heaven—and that includes anyone in heaven, not just those who have been canonized—can pray for us, just as those on earth can do.

The *Catechism of the Catholic Church* assures us of the prayers of the saints: "The witnesses who have preceded us into the kingdom," it says, "especially those whom the Church recognizes as saints, share in the living tradition of prayer by the example of their lives, the transmission of their writings, and their prayer today. They contemplate God, praise him and constantly care for those whom they have left on earth.... Their intercession is their most exalted service to God's plan. We can and should ask them to intercede for us and for the whole world."

C.S. Lewis, although an Anglican, understood the doctrine of the communion of saints. In his book *Letters to Malcolm (Chiefly About Prayer)*, he asked, "If you can ask for the prayers of the living, why should you not ask for the prayers of the dead?" He hoped that his church, the Church of England, would not canonize people because he thought it would cause divisions. However, he practiced praying *with* the saints, including "our own dear dead," and hoped that their voices might be more effective than his own by itself might be.

Lewis's inclusion of "our own dear dead" makes me wonder how many people pray *to*, as well as *for*, their parents or close friends. After all, anyone who gets to heaven is a saint and those who knew us intimately here on earth would naturally be the ones who would be most interested in interceding for us in heaven. We can intercede for them in case they're still being purified in purgatory and they can intercede for us. That, after all, is what the doctrine of the communion of saints is all about.

You, St. Francis, wrote: "Choose certain particular saints whose lives you can best appreciate and imitate and in whose intercession you may have particular confidence. The saint whose name you bear was already assigned to you at baptism." I'm sure that most people have their favorite saints to whom they pray. For some, like me, they're our patron saints. I've already written why, as a writer with the name John Francis, I chose John the Evangelist and you, St. Francis, as my patron saints instead of other saints with those names.

I have to tell you, though (and it's certainly no secret from you), that my favorite saint is St. Thomas More. He was a man that most of us can emulate, especially married men. He is possibly the best example of a man who could be eminently successful in secular life while still maintaining the religious practices that can make anyone a saint. He was one of the best authors of the Renaissance. A chronology of his published works lists 30 writings, and "The Complete Works of Thomas More," published by Yale University Press, consists of 15 large volumes. He was also a husband and a father who knew what it was like to live in the bedlam of hectic family life. I feel comfortable praying to him as well as to you and St. John the Evangelist.

There are married women saints, too, of course—not only our relatives and friends but also some who were even canonized. Your favorite married woman saint was apparently St. Monica, whom you mention seven times. She, too, of course, is one of those featured in my book *Married Saints.* She is the patron saint of all mothers as well as of married women, housewives, alcoholics, and those who are victims of infidelity.

You, St. Francis, lived on earth well before St. Thérèse of Lisieux, but I have an idea that you are great friends in heaven. You are both Doctors of the Church, of course, and I'm sure you approved of her "little way." She stressed finding holiness in the ordinary circumstances of everyday life—in whatever we are doing— and that's quite similar to what you wrote about developing a devout life in any occupation or way of life. St. Thérèse is one of the favorite saints of many people today. Before her death, she said, "I want to spend my heaven doing good on earth" so it's no wonder that people like to pray for her intercession.

Another favorite is St. Francis of Assisi, and you can understand that since you mentioned him seven times, too. St. Anthony of Padua is popular, also, as people pray to him when they have lost something, and St. Jude has become the patron of lost causes.

I must say, though, that some devotions to saints at least border on superstition if they're not totally superstitious. Novenas to St. Jude that promise the answer to prayers if the one doing the praying distributes a certain number of copies of the prayer, and then publishes a thank-you in a newspaper after the prayers are answered, come under that category. Catholic newspapers often don't know what to do with people who want to publish ads that contain the promise of assured answers to prayers. They usually forbid the inclusion of the promise and accept ads that simply thank St. Jude for prayers answered.

There is also a superstitious devotion to St. Martha, similar to the one to St. Jude, which tells people that their prayers will be answered if they circulate a certain number of copies of the prayer. This devotion is not only superstitious but also shows biblical ignorance on the part of those promoting the devotion because the instructions state that Martha was the sister of St. Mary Magdalene. No, she wasn't. Martha was the sister of Mary and Lazarus, who lived in Bethany of Judea, near Jerusalem. Mary Magdalene has that name because she came from Magdala in Galilee. Mary Magdalene was the leader of the women who followed Jesus and ministered to him. She was the female counterpart of Peter, the leader of the men. She was the most prominent of Jesus's female disciples since she was mentioned by name by all of the evangelists. Martha, Mary and Lazarus were good friends of Jesus who frequently had him as a guest in their home. They appear only in the Gospel According to St. John.

Before I finish this letter about prayer to saints, let me mention a form of prayer we don't hear much these days—litanies. As I was growing up the Litany of the Blessed Mother and the Litany of All Saints were both popular, but you don't hear them now. That's just an observation, not necessarily a criticism. I guess novenas aren't as popular as they once were either. Perhaps both are considered pre-Vatican II types of devotion.

The Psalms

Dear St. Francis,

Many Catholics have never been taught to appreciate the psalms. That's too bad because these ancient Jewish prayers remain essential to the life of the Catholic Church. Part of a psalm is included in almost every Mass. But too often those at Mass don't pray those psalms with any great devotion.

You, St. Francis, seem to have had a great devotion to the psalms. You didn't instruct Philothea to pray them often, but you quoted various psalms frequently, so you obviously prayed them yourself sufficiently to know them well.

In his keynote address at an international consultation on priestly formation in 1998, Cardinal Godfried Danneels of Belgium said, "For prayer, the foundation is the psalms." He said that he suffered from the fact that so many priests "merely read the psalms. The psalms have never actually entered into their hearts or have had any emotional impact on them."

The psalms were the prayers Jesus prayed. As any good Jewish boy of his time, he probably knew most of the 150 psalms by heart. Even on the cross, he prayed Psalm 22, which begins, "My God, my God, why have you abandoned me?"

St. Thomas More loved the psalms. Some of them were part of his daily prayers, particularly the seven penitential psalms. For night prayer with his family he chose Psalms 51, 25, 67 and 130, the *De Profundis.* Toward the end of his life he wrote an extended commentary on Psalm 91, and while in prison he collected verses from 31 psalms to form one powerful prayer he could pray in his cell. His last prayer was Psalm 51.

The *Catechism of the Catholic Church* calls the psalms "the masterwork of prayer in the Old Testament." They were composed from the time of David until after the exile to Babylon but not as late as the Maccabean period, about 165 B.C.

Most of the psalms were composed for liturgical worship, although they are both personal and communal. Today, anyone who prays the Liturgy of the Hours prays almost all of the psalms over a four-week period, but some are prayed more often than others are.

The one prayed most frequently is Psalm 95, since it is the Invitatory Psalm, a call to praise God, the first prayer of each day.

Praise of God is the most common theme of the psalms. Indeed, the psalms were collected into five books of the Psalter, which means "Praises." But there are many other forms of prayer, too: lament, contrition, petition, thanksgiving. Some, too, reflect Jewish history and theology.

They usually are simple prayers and they sound spontaneous, but some are literary masterpieces, especially Psalm 119. By far the longest psalm in the Psalter, it has 176 verses. It is an acrostic: its twenty-two stanzas (of eight verses each) are in the order of the Hebrew alphabet and each verse within a stanza starts with the same letter.

St. Ambrose wrote, "A psalm is a blessing on the lips of the people, praise of God, the assembly's homage, a general acclamation, a word that speaks for all, the voice of the Church, a confession of faith in song."

St. Pope Pius X had a great love of the psalms. He wrote: "Who could fail to be moved by those many passages in the psalms which set forth so profoundly the infinite majesty of God, his omnipotence, his justice and goodness and clemency, too deep for words, and all the other infinite qualities of his that deserve our praise? Who could fail to be aroused to the same emotions by the prayers of thanksgiving to God for blessings received, by the petitions, so humble and confident, for blessings still awaited, by the cries of a soul in sorrow for sin committed? Who would not be fired with love as he looks on the likeness of Christ, the redeemer, here so lovingly foretold?"

Let me briefly describe 15 of my favorite psalms, ten percent of the total 150, in numerical order. Other people might have different favorites, but these are the ones that seem most meaningful to me.

Psalm 8 celebrates both God's majesty and human dignity. It describes how awesome God is, marveling at his creation and how he has made us mortals little less than gods, giving us rule over all things of earth.

Psalm 15 is a short five verses that asks, "Who may abide in God's tent?" The answer is: those who walk without blame, do what is right, speak the truth, do not slander, and several other things. It's a reminder to me what I must do to "abide in God's tent."

Psalm 23 ("The Lord is my shepherd") is probably familiar to most people. It's a comforting psalm, assuring me that God is always at my side, no matter what.

Psalm 27 seems to flow from Psalm 23. It tells me to trust in God because he will never forsake me.

Psalm 42 is a longing, a thirst, for God. This is a sentiment I want to become a part of me. (Psalm 63 expresses the same sentiments.)

Psalm 51 is the most famous of the seven penitential psalms. The Church includes it in the Liturgy of the Hours every Friday morning (except on feasts or solemnities). I ask God to have mercy on me and to blot out my offenses. It goes on to pray for a clean heart and a steadfast spirit.

Psalm 84 is similar to Psalm 42 in that both express a longing for God. Psalm 84 says that the one praying is yearning and pining for the court of the Lord.

Psalm 90 reminds me of God's eternity and the shortness of my life. It says that the span of our lives is seventy years or eighty for those who are strong, and that they pass away quickly. It asks God to grant me wisdom to understand the shortness of my life and to grant success to the works of my hands.

Psalm 91 assures me that there is security under God's protection. It's a good night prayer, which the Church includes as part of Compline in the Liturgy of the Hours.

Psalm 100 is a short (five verses) hymn of

praise and thanksgiving. It was originally an invitation to people to enter the temple to offer thank offerings to God.

Psalm 103 is a prayer of thanksgiving, but it also praises God's goodness. It reminds me not to forget God's gifts. However, as Psalm 90 does, it says that the days of our lives are like flowers that bloom but are blown away by the wind.

Psalm 130 is a prayer for pardon and mercy, another of the seven penitential psalms. It begins: "Out of the depths I call to you, Lord; Lord, hear my cry! May your ears be attentive to my cry for mercy."

Psalm 139 is, I believe, the most intimate psalm. It acknowledges that God knows all about me because it was he who created me and who knows my most intimate thoughts. It's a reminder of God's omnipresence and omniscience.

Psalm 148 is one of two psalms of praise toward the end of the Psalter. It's a good one to use at the beginning of one's prayers. It summons all creation to praise God—angels, hosts, sun, moon, shining stars, highest heavens, sea monsters, lightning and hail, snow and clouds, stormy winds, mountains and hills, trees, animals, and all peoples, young and old alike.

Psalm 150 is another psalm of praise; this

one is best recited at the end of one's prayers. In six verses, it calls us to praise God for his mighty deeds and his great majesty, and it says we should praise him with horns, harp, lyre, tambourines and dance, flutes and strings, and crashing cymbals.

I don't feel I can finish this letter, though, without saying that, in my opinion, some of the palms are not appropriate for one's prayer life. The Church recognizes this in its Liturgy of the Hours. Someone who prays the entire Liturgy of the Hours over a four-week period will pray at least parts of 146 psalms. They will not pray Palms 54, 58, 83 and 109. They either contain accusations against God himself or curse antagonists. A few psalms seem to be worthy prayers but suddenly veer towards sentiments we would consider unworthy. Psalm 18, for example, is a long psalm of thanksgiving to God. But while praising God for his help in battle, the one praying recounts how he pursued and killed his foes, having no mercy on them even when they cried to the Lord.

Psalm 149 says that God takes delight in his people and the faithful should rejoice in their glory. But then it switches to the sentiment that, with praise of God on their lips, the faithful should bring retribution to the nations and punishment on the peoples.

These were apparently praiseworthy sentiments at the time the psalms were written, but not today. What to do about them? I simply don't pray the offending verses; I skip over them. I pray the psalms with which I'm comfortable.

Scripture and Prayer

Dear St. Francis,

In your *Introduction to the Devout Life*, St. Francis, you wrote: "Be devoted to the word of God whether you hear it in familiar conversation with spiritual friends or in sermons. Always listen to it with attention and reverence; make good use of it; do not let it fall to earth but take it into your heart like a precious balm."

Someone else (I forget now who) said, "When we pray we speak to God. When we read the Bible God speaks to us." That's how we have a conversation, I guess. Actually, I think you agree with me that God also speaks to us in the silence of our meditation or contemplation as well as in spiritual reading, but certainly the sentiment in that quotation is good.

Vatican II's Dogmatic Constitution on Divine Revelation, *Dei Verbum*, made it clear that God is the author of Sacred Scripture: "The divinely revealed realities, which are contained and presented in the text of Sacred Scripture, have been written down under the inspiration of the Holy Spirit." So we should indeed think of reading the Bible as God speaking to us.

Catholics have not always been known as great Bible readers. Indeed, many older Catholics will still say that they were taught in their Catholic schools that reading the Bible could be dangerous to their faith. This was a holdover from the efforts Pope Pius X made to combat modernism, especially Scripture studies that tried to show that the Bible could not be read as a literal account of historical events. Until the middle of the twentieth century, future priests were taught a biblical fundamentalism that tried to prove, for example, that Jonah could have lived inside a whale. Fortunately, those days are gone and the Church no longer teaches a literal sense of all Scripture. But those years when Scripture scholars were suspect made Catholics believe that they shouldn't read the Bible.

Fortunately, that is no longer true and more Catholics than ever before are now becoming familiar with the word of God expressed in the Bible. We still have a long way to go to catch up with some of our Protestant neighbors, but we're getting there.

But, of course, Catholics have never been wholly ignorant of Scripture because we listen to the reading of some of it at every Mass. That includes the Old Testament as well as the New Testament because the Church believes that the books of the Old Testament were divinely inspired, too. The early Fathers of the Church (Augustine, John Chrysostom, Gregory of Nyssa, Origen, among others) taught that the Old Testament is a symbolic anticipation of the New Testament. *Dei Verbum* said that the books of the Old Testament "are a storehouse of sublime teaching on God and of sound wisdom on human life, as well as a wonderful treasury of prayers; in them, too, the mystery of our salvation is present in a hidden way." Many of those prayers, of course, are the psalms.

If the Old Testament presents the mystery of our salvation in a hidden way, the New Testament does so explicitly because its central object is Jesus Christ, God's Son made incarnate. And at the heart of all the Scriptures are the Gospels because, again quoting *Dei Verbum*, "they are our principal source for the life and teaching of the Incarnate Word, our Savior."

But this letter isn't meant to be about Scripture itself, just about the use of Scripture in our prayers.

It was the Benedictine monks who introduced what is known as *lectio divina*, the meditative reading of Scripture or the writings of the Fathers of the Church. In your instructions about meditation, you advised Philothea to picture in her imagination the entire scene that she wanted to meditate on. What better way is there to do that than to read about that scene in the Scriptures?

Jesus made it easy for us, too, because he taught much of the time with parables. He told stories to make his point. These stories are great for meditation purposes. We can picture the scene that Jesus describes, focus on the message Jesus was trying to teach with the parable, think about how it applies to our lives, and resolve to act on it.

There are three principal parables on prayer in St. Luke's Gospel: the friend who persists in asking for bread for another friend until the man gets it for him, the widow who persists in pestering a dishonest judge until he grants what she wants, and the Pharisee and the tax collector. The first two invite us to pray with persistence and patience and the third is the humble prayer, "God, be merciful to me a sinner."

Jesus teaches us to pray not only with those parables, and not only with the words of the *Our Father*, but by his own actions. Luke's Gospel shows Jesus praying before every decisive moment, often spending the night in prayer in solitude. Luke doesn't give us any details of those prayers but we can imagine

Jesus asking his Father for the strength and wisdom to carry out the Father's will and to complete his mission on earth.

The Gospels do give us the details of some of Jesus's prayers, though. In Chapter 11 of Matthew's Gospel and Chapter 10 of Luke's, Jesus praises the Father for hiding things from the wise and learned and revealing them to the childlike. Another prayer is one that he prays before raising Lazarus from the dead. Here he thanks the Father for hearing him. The interesting thing here is that Jesus prays that prayer before he calls Lazarus to come out of the tomb. He says that he knows that the Father always hears him; but he also explains that he said this so the crowd would believe that the Father sent him.

Jesus's longest prayer comprises all of Chapter 17 in John's Gospel. Since the sixteenth century, this prayer has been called the "high priestly prayer" of Jesus because it embraces the whole economy of creation and salvation. Many phrases are reminiscent of the *Our Father* as Jesus says that he glorified the Father's name, accomplished the will of the Father, and prays that his apostles will be delivered from evil.

Jesus prayed that prayer as a great high priest, but hours later he prayed another prayer while he was in anguish in the Garden of Gethsemane. Knowing that he would soon suffer tremendously and die the cruel death of crucifixion, he prayed, "Father, if you are willing, take this cup away from me; still, not my will but yours be done." He desperately wanted to escape what was coming and asked God to arrange things so he wouldn't have to die, even though he had known that it was going to happen. God did not grant that prayer because it was not in accordance with his plans. We can learn from this that God will not always grant what we pray for and that we should accept our afflictions submissively when they are God's will.

Besides the Gospels, St. Paul's letters provide an endless supply of topics on which to meditate. My favorite reading in all of Scripture is in the second chapter of St. Paul's Letter to the Philippians: "Though he was in the form of God, etc." It sums up the awesome mysteries of the Incarnation and Redemption—that, although Jesus was God he actually humbled himself to become a human and then not only died but did so through the horrible torture of crucifixion, and all for each one of us.

Sacred Scriptures, of course, are not the only spiritual reading that can guide us in meditation. You, St. Francis, recognized that and, in the same section in which you advised Philothea to be devoted to the word of God, you told her to "always have at hand some approved book of devotion" and you mentioned thirteen possibilities that were apparently particularly popular during your day. (I have to tell you, though, that I'm completely unfamiliar with some of the authors you mentioned— Gerson, Denis the Carthusian, Louis of Blois, Granada, Stella, Arias, Pinelli, and Du Pont.) I'm surprised, though, that you didn't recommend the writings of the Fathers and Doctors of the Church.

You said, too, that Philothea "should also read stories and lives of the saints for there, as in a mirror, you can see a picture of the Christian life and adapt their deeds to your use in keeping with your vocation." You yourself especially had great admiration for Sts. Teresa of Avila, Ignatius of Loyola, Charles Borromeo, Louis and Bernard.

Today there are probably more lives of the saints, as well as many more spiritual books of all kinds, than there were in your day, St. Francis, and many of them can help us in meditative prayer. There are also monthly periodicals with commentary on parts of the Bible and suggestions for beginning a meditation.

But perhaps the best source of readings from the Doctors of the Church and from other saints whose feasts are celebrated throughout the liturgical year is the Office of Readings. These readings are part of the Liturgy of the

Hours so they are read as part of liturgical prayer and I doubt that many people meditate over them for prolonged periods of time. But, other than the words of God himself, what better meditation guide can there be than those the Church has recognized as its greatest teachers?

Discerning God's Will

Dear St. Francis,

You know, St. Francis, I think that the most important thing you wrote in *Introduction to the Devout Life* was buried as the last sentence in a long paragraph in Section 13 of the Fourth Part of the book. You wrote: "True devotion consists in a constant, resolute, prompt, and active will to do whatever we know is pleasing to God." Why didn't you put that up front somewhere so it would have a better chance of getting your readers' attention?

If that is what true devotion consists in, it seems to follow that our constant prayer should be to be able to discern what is pleasing to God. And what is pleasing to God is to do his will— "Thy will be done on earth as it is in heaven." God has given each of us a unique job to do, and unique talents with which to do it, and it's up to us to figure out what that is. It's our vocation in life.

We are accustomed to hearing about vocations in connection with the priesthood and religious life, as when we are asked to pray for "more vocations." But that's not the only meaning. The word "vocation" comes from the same root as "vocal" or "vocabulary." It has to do with the voice or sound. Simply put, in the Christian life, a vocation is a call from God himself to follow a certain course of action in life. That call doesn't always come in loud and clear. Isaiah, for example, found it in a small whisper after not finding it in a windstorm or an earthquake. For us, it usually isn't even a whisper.

I think that we all have many vocations—many calls from God. All of us are called, above all, to obey the two great commandments: First, you shall love the Lord your God with all your heart, with all your being, with all your strength, and with all your mind; and second, you shall love your neighbor as yourself.

Then God calls us to a particular state in life, whether that be to the priesthood, the religious life, marriage, or the single state in the world. Once we make the decision to accept God's call to that state of life, he calls us to something more specific. In the case of a priest, for example, he calls some to be parish priests, others to be teachers, still others to be missionaries or chaplains. And the same is true for lay people in secular society.

Our particular vocation as lay people is to Christianize the temporal order since we live in the temporal order more than priests and religious do. The Second Vatican Council's Decree on the Apostolate of the Laity tells us that it's we laity who "must take on the renewal of the temporal order as (our) own special obligation."

That decree goes on to point out that lay spirituality "will take its particular character from the circumstances of one's state in life (married and family life, celibacy, widowhood), from one's state of health and from one's professional and social activity. Whatever the circumstances, each one has received suitable talents and these should be cultivated, as should also the personal gifts he or she has from the Holy Spirit."

Furthermore, God doesn't make just one call and leave it at that. He calls us to do different things at different stages of our lives. In my case, for example, I'm convinced that God called me be a husband and a father. Then he called me to work for his Church in the Catholic press, both as a way of supporting my wife and children and as a way of serving his Church. Furthermore, he called me to do that in different capacities during my career, sometimes as a publisher and sometimes as an editor. And now, I'm still convinced, he has called me to continue to write about religious matters as my way of carrying out my vocations.

No matter where we happen to be in our lives, we must keep asking ourselves, in our prayers, "What does God want me to do *now*? What is he calling me to do *now*?"

Father Henri Nouwen was one of the most popular authors of Catholic spiritual books in modern times. His thirty-seven books, plus a couple published after his death in 1996, were usually short, and therefore inviting, and they dealt with very human subjects: grief, prayer, spiritual living, love. Several of the books were spiritual journals.

There was a great restlessness about Nouwen. He was a priest and an author, a public speaker and a retreat leader, but he constantly wrote in his spiritual journals that he was always searching for his vocations (in the plural). He taught theology at Notre Dame, spent time in a Trappist monastery, returned to teaching at Yale, lived among the poor in Guatemala, taught some more at Harvard, and ended up doing pastoral work in an organization in Canada that provides homes for the mentally and physically handicapped. During all this time he continued to write spiritual books. He never did discern just one vocation, but he continued throughout his life to ask what God wanted him to do.

All of us must do that.

Nouwen distinguished between vocation and career. "A career disconnected from a vocation divides," he wrote; "a career that expresses obedience to our vocation is the concrete way of making our unique talents available to the community."

That is how we discern our vocations, by prayerfully assessing our unique talents and discovering how God wants us to use them. It's fortunate that God doesn't want us all to do the same thing. We all must be very frank with ourselves in discerning our strengths and our weaknesses, the particular talents God has given us. I've always found St. Paul's teachings about the Mystical Body consoling. He tells us that we all can't do the same thing because God has given each of us different gifts.

Mother Teresa once made that same point when she told me and some other journalists I was with: "You cannot do what I do, but I cannot do what you do. Each of us has his or her own work to do. The important thing is that we do something beautiful for God." She went on to tell us that, as journalists, it was our obligation to write the truth. We were in Jerusalem at the time and she told us that God had brought us to the Holy Land to learn the truth about what was happening there, and then he was calling us to write the truth—something, she said, that we could do but she could not do.

St. Francis, I like the way you tied prayer and vocation together: "You must accustom yourself to know how to pass from prayer to all the various duties your vocation and state of life rightly and lawfully require of you, even though they appear far different from the affections you received in prayer. I mean that the lawyer must be able to pass from prayer to pleading cases, the merchant to commerce, and the married woman to her duties as wife and her household tasks with so much ease and tranquillity that their minds are not disturbed." One thing, though: today that "married woman" might also be the lawyer or the merchant.

One of the things those lawyers, merchants or married women must discern through their prayers is how God is calling them to evangelize the world. The Second Vatican Council made it clear in its Decree on the Apostolate of Lay People that every member of Christ's Mystical Body is called "to spread the kingdom of Christ over all the earth for the glory of God the Father, to make all men partakers in redemption and salvation, and through them to establish the right relationship of the entire world to Christ." The decree emphasized that the lay apostolate is carried out "in the midst of the world and of secular affairs" and that "men, working in harmony, should renew the temporal order and make it increasingly more perfect: such is God's design for the world."

This was reemphasized in October of 1987 when Pope John Paul II called the Synod on the Laity, after which the pope issued the apostolic exhortation *Christifideles Laici*. He laid out his vision of a laity fully living its mission to society and culture. He was emphatic when he said, "It is not permissible for anyone to remain idle." He said that the sanctification of the world—society, culture, the workplace—is the distinctive vocation of the laity. Business, the professions, the creative arts, the media, and politics are, for the pope, all venues in which Christians live the universal call to holiness. To put teeth in what he said, he then established the Pontifical Council for the Laity and charged it with the responsibility to promote the lay mission in the world.

We can't all do the same thing but we all must do something. It's through prayer that we can discern God's will for us at this particular stage of our lives. And once we discern God's will for us, we must pray for the courage and ability to do it.

Difficulties in Prayer

Dear St. Francis,

The *Catechism of the Catholic Church* says that prayer "always presupposes effort." Then it's even stronger when it says: "Prayer is a battle." We have to fight constantly against ourselves and, as the *Catechism* says, "against the wiles of the tempter who does all he can to turn man [and woman, I presume] away from prayer, away from union with God."

You understood that, St. Francis. You told Philothea, "Sometimes you will find yourself deprived and destitute of all feelings of devotion and your soul will seem like a barren, sterile desert where there is no path or road leading to God, nor any water of grace to refresh you because of the aridity that now seems to threaten it with complete and absolute desolation." Boy, did you understand it!

C.S. Lewis also understood it. "Prayer is irksome," he wrote. "An excuse to omit it is never unwelcome. When it is over, this casts a feeling of relief and holiday over the rest of the day. We are reluctant to begin. We are delighted to finish." And he cites the following to show that this feeling is universal: "The fact that prayers are constantly set as penances tells its own tale."

Obviously, this isn't as it should be. It should be a delight to have a conversation with God. And we know that it is a delight for the mystics who go into ecstasy during their prayers. Just to be in God's presence should thrill us. That is, after all, what we are looking forward to spending eternity doing—living in God's presence. Why does it seem like a penance now and what should we do about it?

The answer, of course, is that we haven't yet been perfected. After we get our spiritual bodies we won't be afflicted with all the stuff we have to endure with our physical bodies, with all their limitations. Now we're preoccupied with indulging our physical pleasures, those things that delight our senses. Once we have our spiritual bodies we will no longer be concerned about our physical senses.

Until then, though, prayer is a battle. The battle is to confront the difficulties we experience in prayer. The *Catechism* calls it failure in prayer, but I think the word "failure" is too harsh. "Difficulties" is strong enough.

Unless I'm completely different from other people, I'd say that distractions are the most common difficulty in prayer. But I already discussed distractions in an earlier letter, so I won't repeat myself here. Rather, let me turn to another difficulty: dryness. That's when our heart seems separated from God, when we have no desire for spiritual things and our faith is tempted. It's not only we ordinary people who experience that either. Many canonized saints experienced it.

This dryness seems to come primarily in meditation or contemplative prayer, and you, St. Francis, had quite a bit to say about it. You advised Philothea that, if she should happen to find no joy or comfort in meditation to "open your heart's door to words of vocal prayer." In other words, ask God for his help.

"At other times," you wrote, "turn to some spiritual book and read it attentively until your mind is awakened and restored within you." And if this doesn't work, you said not to worry about it.

I'm going to quote another of your passages at length because it expresses so well what our attitude toward prayer should be. You wrote: "We ought to approach holy prayer purely and simply to do our duty and testify to our fidelity. If it pleases his Divine Majesty to speak to us and aid us by his holy inspirations and interior consolations, it is certainly a great honor and the sweetest of delights. But if it does not please him to grant this favor and he leaves without speaking to us, just as if he did not see us at all or we were not in his presence, we must not leave on that account. On the contrary, we must remain with a respectful and devotional bearing in the presence of his sovereign goodness. He will unfailingly be pleased with our patience and take note of our diligence and perseverance, so that when we again come before him he will favor and help us by his consolations and enable us to see how sweet is holy prayer. Yet if he does not do so, let us be content that it is the very greatest honor for us to stand before him and in his sight."

In other words, we must persevere in our prayers in season and out of season, when we feel like praying and when we don't feel like praying. Perhaps in God's eyes (where it's most important) the prayers we say when we least feel like praying are really our best prayers.

Spiritual writers identify another difficulty in prayer as *acedia*, which the catechism defines as "a form of depression due to lax ascetical practice, decreasing vigilance, carelessness of heart" but which my dictionary says is merely spiritual torpor or apathy. This, I think, we must overcome through willpower.

Another reason for difficulties in prayer,

of course, is alluded to in that quotation with which I opened this letter: the wiles of the tempter who tries to turn us away from prayer. Often it is the devil who suggests to us that we really would get more out of that television program than we could from prayer. He would like to do anything that keeps us away from our conversation with God. He doesn't have to tempt us with sinful inclinations, just convince us that something else is more important. He's the one who convinces us that prayer is "irksome," in C.S. Lewis's words, and makes us glad to get it over with.

If prayer is a battle against the devil, perhaps one of our greatest weapons is the prayer to St. Michael the archangel in which we ask him to "defend us in battle. Be our safeguard against the wiles and snares of the devil."

Finding Balance in Life

Dear St. Francis,

I had to smile a bit, St. Francis, when I read the section of *Introduction to the Devout Life* that answered two objections to what you had written. The first objection was that the exercises and counsels you set out are so numerous that anyone who wants to practice them must do nothing else. That's the part that made me smile. I feel sure that the same thing can be said about everything I've written about prayer in these letters.

Your answer was that it's true that the exercises would constitute our entire occupation if they were all performed every day but that it is not necessary to perform them except at the proper time and place, each one according to the opportunity for it. That's the way it is with the various prayers I've written about in these letters.

It is possible, though, for someone to make regular prayer an important part of his or her daily routine. You used one of your favorite saints to give an example of someone who did exactly that. You wrote: "St. Louis, a king who was admirable in both war and peace and administered justice and managed his affairs with unrivalled care, heard two Masses every day, said Vespers and Compline with his chaplain, made his meditation, visited hospitals, confessed and took the discipline every Friday, heard many sermons, and held many spiritual conferences. With all that, he never let pass a single occasion of promoting the public good without improving it and diligently putting it into effect."

The other objection you answered was that you assumed that Philothea had the gift of mental prayer, whereas not everyone has that gift. Unfortunately, that seems to be true. I recall attending Mass in a parish not my own while visiting one of our children for a few days. One priest said Mass the first day and a different priest the next day. The first priest, during his homily, told the congregation that he had never had the patience to sit still long enough to meditate, that it seemed like a waste of time to him when he could be doing something he considered more important. The next day the second priest gave his homily on prayer (the Gospel reading was Christ teaching the apostles the *Our Father*) and he spoke about how important meditation and contemplation were to him. I already knew that because I had come to church early enough to meditate for a while before Mass and the priest was sitting in a front pew doing the same. This priest even had all of us sit quietly in contemplation for a couple minutes at the end of his homily. Two priests with completely different personalities were serving in that parish.

That first priest, obviously a restless and energetic activist, certainly prayed; he led us in prayer during that Mass. He simply never learned to meditate. Don't we all know many people like that, people who have to be doing something all the time? I'm willing to bet that they are in the majority among Catholics if we were to assume that those who arrive just in time for Mass (or even a couple minutes late) don't like to "waste" a moment and are the type who don't have the gift of mental prayer. That might be an unfair assumption, of course, because it's possible that some of them meditate at home, but I wonder.

Anyway, St. Francis, your answer to that objection was that, while it is true that not everyone has the gift of mental prayer, almost all people, "even the most ignorant," can have it provided they have good guides and are willing to take as many pains to obtain it as it deserves. Frankly, I thought you were a little harsh, throwing in that phrase "even the most ignorant." I don't think intelligence has anything to do with it. That priest who told the congregation that he didn't have the patience for meditation is certainly an intelligent man. He's just the "A" type who has to be doing something all the time. And I for one am not going to say that he isn't just as close to God as the priest who practices contemplation on a regular basis.

I believe that prayer is important or I wouldn't be writing these letters about it. But Jesus didn't tell us that we would be judged by how well we prayed. He told us that we would be judged by how well we performed the corporal works of mercy—feeding the hungry, giving drink to the thirsty, clothing the naked, etc. I think that people who do those things on a regular basis are as close to God as those who devote much of their time to prayer. I don't recall Jesus explicitly telling us that only those who pray a great deal will enter heaven. I do recall him saying explicitly, in the twenty-fifth chapter of Matthew's Gospel, that those who do not perform the corporal works of mercy "will go off to eternal punishment"!

Having said that, though, I will again hearken back to the consoling letters of St. Paul who told us that, as part of the Mystical Body, we are not all expected to do the same thing. We are not all called to serve food to the hungry at soup kitchens. Perhaps feeding our families or providing warm clothing for our children during the winter is sufficient to get us off the hook.

The real answer is that there should be a balance in our lives. Books on the lives of saints are full of stories about activist men and women who received their inspiration through meditation or contemplation. Your own life, St. Francis, is an example. You and your cousin, Louis de Sales, had a tough time of it while working among the Calvinists in Chablais. That's where you began your ministry of writing leaflets about Catholic doctrine, comparing it to the teachings of Calvinism. You spent a lot of time laboriously copying those little papers by hand and distributing them by any means available. You also preached in the marketplace and had public debates with some of the Calvinist leaders in the area. You were working, but you were also praying. You found the necessary balance in your life, and that's what we all must search for.

At the end of *Introduction to the Devout Life*, St. Francis, you admonished Philothea to persevere in the devout life because, as you said, "Our days glide away; death is at the gate." Look up to heaven, you said, and look down into hell and do not cast yourself into it for the sake of fleeting things. I think that is very much like the way St. Thomas More felt. The Scripture quotation, "What does it profit a man if he gains the whole world but suffers the loss of his soul?" was very real to him. He wrote that even the greatest of earthly pleasures is "little, simple, short, and suddenly past." Why, he asked, would any sane person buy a momentary pleasure for an eternity of pain?

We must keep our eyes on heaven. That's where we hope to spend an eternity of happiness, praising and glorifying God. While still here on earth, let us practice doing that through our prayers.

Thank you, St. Francis, for teaching us how to do that.

ST PAULS

This book was produced by St. Pauls/Alba House, the Society of St. Paul, an international religious congregation of priests and brothers dedicated to serving the Church through the communications media.

For information regarding this and associated ministries of the Pauline Family of Congregations, write to the Vocation Director, Society of St. Paul, P.O. Box 189, 9531 Akron-Canfield Road, Canfield, Ohio 44406-0189. Phone (330) 702-0359; or E-mail: spvocationoffice@aol.com or check our internet site, www.albahouse.org